Aviation Elite Units

Jagdgeschwader 2 'Richthofen'

Aviation Elite Units • 1

Jagdgeschwader 2 'Richthofen'

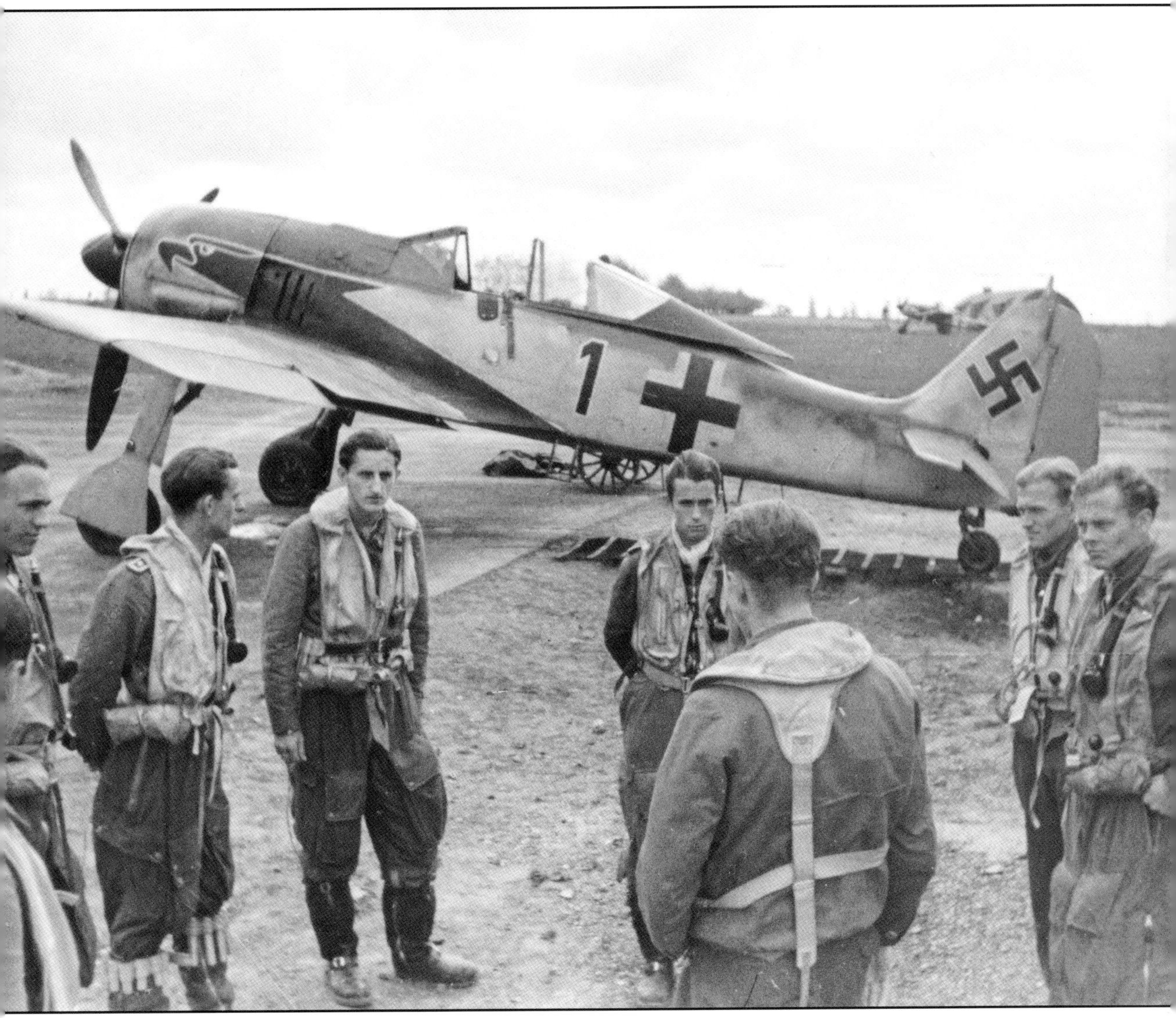

John Weal

Series editor Tony Holmes

Front cover
After cutting their teeth on short-range cross-Channel operations during the late summer/early autumn of 1942, the pioneer heavy bomber groups of the Eighth Air Force began to venture further afield. Their next targets included the German navy's U-Boat pens along the French Atlantic coast.

On 23 November 1942, for the fifth time in the space of a fortnight, elements of the embryonic 'Mighty Eighth' hit St Nazaire. Solid undercast prevented all but nine B-17Fs of the 91st and 306th Bomb Groups from reaching their objective. Those that made it to the target were met by a frightening new tactic on the part of the Luftwaffe's fighter defences – frontal attack!

The originator of the head-on assault, Hauptmann Egon Mayer (recently-appointed *Gruppen-kommandeur* of III./JG 2) led his Fw 190s through the B-17 formation in the most successful pass yet carried out against the still relatively inexperienced heavy bomber crews. Four Flying Fortresses were claimed destroyed, including one by Mayer himself, for the loss of a single Focke-Wulf fighter.

In this specially-commissioned artwork by Jim Laurier, Mayer's 'White Double Chevron', with his port wingman in close attendance, is seen scything through the leading section of B-17s. Egon Mayer would add 24 more USAAF 'heavies' to his score, which made him the foremost *Viermot-Experte* of the Luftwaffe at the time of his death in action against P-47s in March 1944

Back cover
A clutch of senior officers from II./JG 2 pose at the *Gruppe's* Neumünster base on the North Sea coast in April 1940. The aircraft forming the backdrop for this photograph is the Bf 109E-1 'White 1' of 4./JG 2's *Staffelkapitän* (seen standing second from left), Leutnant Hans Hahn

First published in Great Britain in 2000 by Osprey Publishing
Elms Court, Chapel Way, Botley, Oxford, OX2 9LP, UK

ISBN 1 84176 046 3

Edited by Tony Holmes
Page design by Mark Holt
Cover Artwork by Jim Laurier
Aircraft Profiles by John Weal
Origination by Grasmere Digital Imaging, Leeds, UK
Printed in Hong Kong through Bookbuilders

04 05 06 07 08 10 9 8 7 6 5 4 3

ACKNOWLEDGEMENTS
The author would like to thank the following publishers and individuals for allowing access to their archives, and for their generous help in providing information and photographs.

In England – Aerospace Publishing Ltd, Chris Goss, Michael Payne, Dr Alfred Price, Jerry Scutts, Robert Simpson and W J A 'Tony' Wood.

In Germany – Motorbuch Verlag, Wolfgang Fischer, Col Thomas C Fosnacht, Werner Kock, Genltn Bruno Maass (deceased), Walter Matthiesen, Holger Nauroth, Heinz J Nowarra (deceased) and Herbert Ringlstetter.

EDITOR'S NOTE
To make this new series as authoritative as possible, the Editor would be interested in hearing from any individual who may have relevant photographs, documentation or first-hand experiences relating to aircrews, and their aircraft, of the various theatres of war. Any material used will be credited to its original source. Please write to Tony Holmes, 16 Sandilands, Chipstead, Sevenoaks, Kent, TN13 2SP, or via e-mail at tony.holmes@osprey-jets.freeserve.co.uk

CONTENTS

THE EARLY YEARS

Die Reklamestaffel Mitteldeutschlands, Deutscher Luftsportverband, eingetragener Verein (Döberitz) (The Central-German Publicity Squadron, German Air-Sports Club Registered Association (Döberitz)) is an imposing enough title in either German or English. But when the unit saddled with this lengthy, if seemingly innocuous, appellation also proves to be the fountain-head from which sprang – either directly or otherwise – almost the entire pre-war fighter, *Zerstörer* and dive-bomber strength of the German Luftwaffe, then it clearly warrants closer scrutiny.

Contrary to long-held belief, the Third Reich's air arm did not rise, phoenix-like, from the ashes the moment Adolf Hitler was elected Chancellor of Germany on 30 January 1933. Although cloaked in a veil of secrecy and official deception, its period of gestation had already been underway for more than a decade under the watchful auspices of the Weimar Republic.

Military aviation had come of age during World War 1. In just four short, cataclysmic years, from 1914 to 1918, the warplane had evolved from a stick-and-string novelty that was largely frowned upon for frightening the cavalry horses, into a deadly weapon of terror and destruction so feared that the victorious allies sought to eradicate entirely Germany's still formidable air forces.

Although the post-war Treaty of Versailles, signed in that palace's great Hall of Mirrors on 28 June 1919, permitted the vanquished foe to retain a token ground army of 100,000 men, it expressly prohibited Germany from keeping a single one of the nearly 20,000 military aircraft still on charge at the close of hostilities.

So all-embracing were the conditions imposed by the Allies that the 75,000 word Treaty, comprising 440 separate articles, required just five sweeping clauses to effectively expunge German military aviation from the post-war European scene. Article 198 of the Treaty stated that Germany was forbidden from maintaining 'either land-based or naval air forces', while Article 202 sought to ensure compliance with the victors' demands by decreeing that all existing military aircraft were to be surrendered to the Allies.

But the Treaty of Versailles was not as watertight as those responsible for its implementation imagined it to be. A number of ploys were used to outwit the officers of the Allied Control Commission. Some 1000 aircraft were reportedly smuggled abroad and sold, others were registered in the technically Free City of Danzig, while still more were quite simply hidden.

Nor was it only in terms of hardware that the Germans sought to circumvent the conditions imposed by the hated *Versailler Diktat*. From its very inception the 100,000-man army permitted by the Treaty had managed surreptitiously to include among its 4000-strong officer corps some 120 ex-World War 1 flyers. And since then ever-increasing numbers of flying personnel had been clandestinely trained, and machines secretly developed, with the connivance of certain foreign governments. Foremost amongst these were undoubtedly the Soviets who, in 1925, placed at Germany's disposal the airfield at Lipetsk, approximately 240 miles (385 km) south of Moscow.

Over the course of the next eight years some 200 pilots and aircrew underwent training at Lipetsk. Not all enjoyed the decidedly spartan and primitive facilities offered by their temporary Russian home. Indeed, new intakes for each six-month course were greeted by a sign which, roughly translated, read 'Welcome to the arse-end of the world'! But without this small, yet invaluable, cadre of experienced officers, which included such later wartime luminaries as Falck, Gentzen, Lützow, Rubensdörffer and Trautloft, it would have been all but impossible to carry out the Luftwaffe's ambitious expansion programmes of the mid-1930s.

In the autumn of 1930 preparations were being made for the activation of a military air arm in the Homeland itself. And by year's end, the first three army flying units proper (as opposed to the thinly-disguised 'civil' flying schools, which had been in operation since 1924) were formed.

Disguised to the outside world as *Reklamestaffeln* (publicity squadrons – this name being deliberately chosen to imply their use for industrial aerial-advertising purposes), the three units were set up at Berlin-Staaken, Fürth, near Nuremberg, and Königsberg in East Prussia. Operating as an integral part of the *Reichsheer*, they were employed on target-towing, artillery spotting, liaison and other allied duties whenever the army embarked upon field manoeuvres.

Spanning the gap between the two World Wars, Robert Ritter von Greim, pictured here wearing the *Pour le Mérite* for his 25 victories in the earlier conflict, was selected to command the new Luftwaffe's first *Jagdgruppe*

The next stage in the Weimar Republic's stealthy reconstruction of an army air force was to have been the creation early in 1933 of a complete *Jagdgeschwader* equipped with Italian Fiat CR 30 fighters. But when this scheme came to naught, the *Reichswehrministerium* had perforce to set its sights a little lower, confining itself instead to the formation of a single *Jagdgruppe* for the coming autumn. Each of the three *Reklamestaffeln* was called upon to contribute to this venture, but it fell to the Berlin-Staaken squadron to provide the working nucleus for the new *Jagdgruppe*, which was to be set up at nearby Döberitz-Elsgrund.

In the event, formal – albeit still clandestine – activation did not take place until 1 April 1934. By this time the National-Socialist Party had been in power for more than a year. But just how unaware the new rulers of Germany had been of the groundwork laid by their predecessors was

***Fliegergruppe* Döberitz was initially equipped with a dozen Arado Ar 65 single-seat fighters, each bearing civilian-style registration**

graphically illustrated by a comment made by Hermann Göring, the newly-appointed Reich Commissar for Aviation, when he was first shown around the secret aviation test centre at Rechlin. 'I had no idea you had progressed so far', he remarked, 'All the better!'

1 April 1934 (coincidentally the RAF's 16th birthday) also marked the covert recognition of the Luftwaffe as a separate arm of the Wehrmacht. Not only had the first operational *Gruppe* been formed, an entire command structure was put in place. Overall control was assumed by Hermann Göring in his new role as *Reichsminister der Luftfahrt* (Minister of Aviation), although this peaceable title was somewhat compromised by his initially retaining the now incongruous rank *of General der Infantrie.*

Under Göring's ministry, Germany was divided into six territorial administrative zones (*Luftkreiskommandos*), and the first tactical command was established. This latter, known as 1. *Fliegerdivision*, was headed by Oberst Hugo Sperrle. It was brought into being by the simple expedient of enlarging, and then dividing, the HQ Staff already assigned to Sperrle in his capacity as *Kommandeur der Heeresflieger* (C-in-C Army Aviation), thereby enabling him to discharge both offices simultaneously.

Although it quickly dispersed with the unwieldy title quoted at the head of this chapter, the new fighter unit preserved some semblance of secrecy by operating under the designation of *Fliegergruppe* (Air Wing) Döberitz. This form of nomenclature, which would remain in force until June 1936, offered no clue as to a *Gruppe's* specific function, nor as to its position within the Luftwaffe organisation as a whole.

The officer selected to command *Fliegergruppe* Döberitz was 41-year-old Major Robert Ritter von Greim, whose military career had begun as a cadet with a Royal Bavarian Railway Battalion in 1911. Transferring to the air arm, he had served with distinction as *Staffelführer* of *Jasta* 34 during World War 1 (see *Osprey Aircraft of the Aces 32 - Albatros Aces of World War 1* for further details). By the end of that conflict he had been awarded the *Pour le Mérite* ('Blue Max'), and was leading *Jagdgruppe* 10.

Now honoured with command of the Third Reich's first fighter *Gruppe*, von Greim set about the task of training it to a high level of proficiency. In this he was ably assisted by his three chosen *Staffelkapitäne*:

Hauptleute Johann Raithel, Hans-Hugo Witt and Hans-Jürgen von Cramon-Taubadel.

Hardly had they begun their own working-up, however, before the *Gruppe* was tasked with two additional duties. One was the training of an entirely separate cadre of personnel in readiness for the activation of a planned second *Jagdgruppe*. The other was to initiate a programme of dive-bombing practice in order to be able to provide qualified pilots for the first of the projected *Stukagruppen*.

Döberitz's initial complement of 12 Arado Ar 65s was patently inadequate to cope with such demands, and by year-end its numbers had been substantially increased. No fewer than 80 Arados were by now in service, these being divided almost equally between the *Gruppe* and the fighter school at Schleissheim, near Munich.

On 26 February 1935 Hitler, Göring and von Blomberg (the latter as Minister of Defence and C-in-C of the Wehrmacht) signed the so-called 'Reichsluftwaffe Decree'. This officially proclaimed the Luftwaffe (although the term 'Reichsluftwaffe' was strictly the more accurate, it never found public favour or entered official usage) as a third, and entirely separate, branch of the armed services. At the same time it finally did away with the all too threadbare veil of secrecy which, for the past decade and a half, had enshrouded Germany's military aviation activities. Far from being a political embarrassment, the emergent Luftwaffe could now be used as a powerful propaganda tool, either to woo potential allies, or to impress traditional foes, as the occasion demanded.

The decree came into effect on 1 March 1935. It was on this date that personnel discarded the garb and insignia of the DLV (the German Air-Sports Association), which they had been wearing since the *Reklamestaffeln's* inception, and changed into the brand new uniform of the Luftwaffe (whose smart collar and tie earned them the disparaging nickname of 'weekend warriors' from some die-hards).

Exactly a fortnight later, on 14 March, and amidst much swastika-beflagged pageantry, *Fliegergruppe* Döberitz was ceremonially paraded before an emotional Führer. In order to instil a sense of continuity and forge links with an illustrious past, the first *Gruppe* of the new Luftwaffe was to assume the mantle of Germany's most famous World War 1 fighter pilot. Henceforth, Hitler declared, the unit would bear the title 'Richthofen';

14 March 1935, and a section from a panoramic montage shows Adolf Hitler, flanked by von Greim and Göring, reviewing the men and machines of the *Fliegergruppe* Döberitz, upon whom he has just conferred the title *'Richthofen'*. Note the newsreel cameramen atop the vehicles following behind

'I announce this edict secure in the knowledge and belief that the *Jagdgeschwader "Richthofen"* – imbued with the lofty ideals of the honour and tradition hereby accorded – will prove itself forever equal, both in spirit and performance, to its holy obligations.'

In the days and weeks that followed, Göring and other high-ranking officers held a series of press conferences. The Döberitz aircraft also made a number of diligently rehearsed public appearances. On 19 March they staged a massed fly-past over the centre of the German capital, a display that was to be repeated on 10 April on the occasion of Göring's marriage to the film actress Emmy Sonnemann. These events afforded the Berlin-based correspondents of the world's press ample opportunity to observe, misinterpret, and pass on to their air-conscious readers disturbing accounts of the Luftwaffe's apparent sudden strength and preparedness.

But one fact was kept carefully concealed from the journalists. The fighter unit at Döberitz was still the only *Jagdgruppe* in the Third Reich's much publicised armoury!

Nor were the media representatives the only ones to be hoodwinked. When asked the current strength of the German air force by Britain's then Foreign Secretary, Sir John Simon, who was on an official visit to Berlin at this time, Hitler calmly replied that it had 'reached parity with Great Britain'!

But moves were already in hand to address the situation as the Luftwaffe now embarked upon the first of an increasingly ambitious series of expansion programmes aimed at strengthening its numbers. Before April was out significant changes had occurred within the ranks of *Fliegergruppe* Döberitz.

Ritter von Greim was appointed to the post of Inspector of Fighters and Dive-Bombers. His place was taken by Major Kurt von Doering, who had been a *Staffelführer* in Manfred Freiherr von Richthofen's original *Jagdgeschwader* Nr.1 back in June 1917. Von Doering immediately lost the experienced leader of his 1. *Staffel* when Johann Raithel was promoted to major and departed for Jüterbog-Damm to activate the long awaited second *Gruppe*.

Two of Raithel's *Staffelkapitäne* were also ex-World War 1 fighter pilots. Major Karl-August von Schönebeck, who had claimed eight Allied machines during the 1914-18 conflict, headed the first *Staffel*. The second went to Major Theo Osterkamp, a 32-victory ex-naval

Major Johann Raithel was the first *Kommandeur* of *Fliegergruppe* Damm

Although these are pre-production machines, the *'Richthofen' Gruppen's* first Heinkel He 51s also wore quasi-civilian 'D' codes as shown here, and – until the autumn of 1935 – the old Imperial red-white-black stripes on the starboard side of the tailfin and rudder

ace who, with von Greim's appointment to a staff position, was now the only active flying member of the fledgling Luftwaffe to sport the coveted *Pour le Mérite*. Raithel's third *Staffel* was taken over by Hauptmann von Kormatzki, a relative youngster in comparison to his two veteran colleagues, who had previously served as Ritter von Greim's adjutant at Döberitz.

In keeping with current policy, Raithel's unit was initially known as *Fliegergruppe* Damm (the cover title *Fliegergruppe* Jüterbog having already been allocated to an on-site supply depot). A good-natured, but intense, rivalry soon sprang up between the two *'Richthofen' Gruppen*, with Döberitz remaining the undisputed showpiece of the Luftwaffe. The station's modern mess hall, or *Kasino*, dominated by a life-sized portrait in oils of the immortal Rittmeister himself, played host to many a dignitary and visiting foreign official.

All the more understandable, therefore, was the satisfaction felt by Raithel's pilots – still roughing it on their as-yet unfinished base outside Jüterbog – when they learned that they had been selected to receive the first production models of Heinkel's new He 51 fighter.

During the summer of 1935 both *Gruppen* converted completely to the Heinkel. And the keen spirit of competition between the two – expressed on one memorable occasion by Raithel's pilots reportedly flying across to Döberitz dressed in full suits of armour to challenge their opposite numbers to a tournament, with the losers to pay the bar bill – ensured that each were soon absolute masters of their new mounts.

On an official level, however, there existed a clear-cut division of labour. Döberitz was responsible for the testing of weapons and ancillary equipment, and for conducting trials with the ground organisation, while Damm was charged with perfecting the tactics of aerial pursuit and interception. The latter unit also undertook experiments related to the proposed introduction of 'heavy' fighter units (the later *Zerstörer*).

After a hectic autumn and winter thus spent, the opening weeks of 1936 were marked by a sudden influx of pilots and machines into Döberitz and, to a lesser extent, Jüterbog-Damm. A political crisis – the first of many to punctuate the latter half of the 1930s – was obviously brewing.

On 24 February a sizeable detachment departed Döberitz for Lippstadt, east of Dortmund. Here, they were joined by a group of pilots straight from the Schleissheim fighter school, who brought with them a number of that establishment's Ar 65s and He 51s so as to form *Fliegergruppe* Lippstadt.

Twelve days later the reason for all the feverish activity of the past few weeks became apparent. On 7 March 1936, in blatant defiance of the provisions laid down in the Treaty of Versailles, Hitler marched his troops into the demilitarised zone of the Rhineland.

All three of the Luftwaffe's *Jagdgruppen* now became involved in a gigantic game of bluff as they spearheaded the Führer's first exercise in sabre-rattling. The two 'Richthofen' units had taken off from Döberitz and Jüterbog-Damm before sunrise. Once aloft, the pilots opened sealed orders which instructed them to land on forward fields just short of the Rhine and 'immediately refuel and cover the advancing ground columns against enemy reconnaissance and attack from the air'.

The *'Richthofen'* pilots demonstrate their growing expertise with these tightly-flown *Ketten* high above Cologne. The unmistakable twin spires of the city's great Gothic cathedral and the River Rhine beyond can just be seen emerging from the early morning mist

Fliegergruppe Döberitz's designated area extended across the Rhineland-Palatinate from Karlsruhe up as far as Koblenz. Raithel's *Fliegergruppe* Damm was to cover the adjoining sector northwards from the Rhine's confluence with the Moselle up to the Ruhr (where the Lippstadt contingent assumed responsibility).

The experiences of Major Osterkamp's *Staffel*, based temporarily at Werl (itself not far from Lippstadt), were typical. For the next three days its pilots spent nearly every waking minute in the air, landing only to refuel, snatch a few hurried mouthfuls of food and a cup of strong coffee, before taking off again.

Appearances were all that mattered – appearances of a strong, powerful and ubiquitous Luftwaffe. On one sortie they would be patrolling in *Staffel* formation low over the rooftops of Aachen. On the next they could be in individual *Ketten* winging high above the twin spires of Cologne cathedral. But always they would return to flaunt their apparent strength along the border zones with France.

And, much to Osterkamp's relief, the bluff worked. Not a single French fighter rose to challenge their presence – which was perhaps just as well, for not one of the *Staffel's* Heinkels, in common with the majority of the Luftwaffe machines committed to this hazardous deception, was armed!

Although it was undoubtedly fortunate for Osterkamp and his fellow pilots that there had been no immediate retaliatory action from either the French – or the British – in the face of this, Hitler's first defiant show of arms, the allies' signal lack of response to such provocation did not bode well for Europe's immediate future.

The success of the Rhineland episode led to three more *Jagdgruppen* quickly being formed. Before March was out another cadre had been hived off, this time from *Fliegergruppe* Damm, to become the resident *Jagdgruppe* at Dortmund. And on 1 April 1936 two further *'Richthofen' Staffeln* were detached (one each from Döberitz and Damm) and transferred to Bernburg and Werl respectively to provide the nuclei for new *Gruppen* at these bases.

Thus, in the space of just five short, but eventful, weeks the two *'Richthofen' Gruppen* had, between them, been instrumental in establishing four completely new *Jagdgruppen*. This trebling of the Luftwaffe's fighter strength led, in turn, to the creation of the first two *Jagdgeschwaderstäbe*.

Not unnaturally, the officers appointed to head these new *Stäbe* – and thereby become the first two *Geschwaderkommodores* of the embryonic *Jagdwaffe* – were the most experienced unit leaders then available: the *Kommandeure* of *Fliegergruppen* Döberitz and Damm. On 1 April 1936 von Döering left Döberitz, and the *'Richthofen'* fold, to assume command of the newly-titled *Jagdgeschwader 'Horst Wessel'* (the later ZG 26) at Dortmund. Major Raithel made the shorter hop from Jüterbog-Damm to Döberitz to take office as *Kommodore* of the *Jagdgeschwader 'Richthofen'*.

The two *Gruppenkommandeur* slots thus made vacant were quickly filled. One of Raithel's erstwhile *Staffelkapitäne* at Damm, Karl-August von Schönebeck, was promoted to take his place, while Major Karl Vieck was transferred in from his duties as a course leader at the Schleissheim fighter school to head the Döberitz *Gruppe*.

Exactly two months after this command reshuffle, on 1 June 1936, the Luftwaffe finally did away with

While the first operational units were showcasing the Luftwaffe to the world, the pre-war training organisation was busy producing a whole new generation of flyers. Seen engrossed in a post-flight debriefing in front of a *Schleiflheim* He 51 trainer, this leutnant instructor (right) seems content enough with his pupil's progress – as well he might, for the fähnrich (officer cadet) on the left is one Egon Mayer, a future *Kommodore* of JG 2

the last vestiges of organisational anonymity by scrapping the generic *Fliegergruppe* title, which had hitherto been applied to all units irrespective of their function. The Luftwaffe had now grown into a force totalling 23 *Gruppen* of all types, and the basic unit would henceforth be the *Geschwader*.

Each *Geschwader* would be identified by a specific three-digit designator. These three digits would indicate respectively (a) the *Geschwader* seniority by role (e.g. fighter, bomber etc.), (b) the actual role itself, and (c) the territorial command in which the *Geschwader* was located.

Under this new system, the *Jagdgeschwader 'Richthofen'* now found itself operating as JG 132 which, to those in the know, revealed it to be the senior fighter *Geschwader* based in the Berlin area – '1' indicated its being the first unit of its kind to be activated, '3' the code for fighters, and '2' referred to *Luftkreiskommando II*, i.e. the Berlin region.

Within the framework of the *Geschwader*, each *Gruppe* was identified by a Roman numeral prefix (and their component *Staffeln*, in turn, by Arabic numeral prefixes). Thus, the *Fliegergruppen* Döberitz and Damm now emerged as I./JG 132 (with 1. to 3. *Staffeln*) and II./JG 132 (4. to 6. *Staffeln*) respectively.

He 51s of the recently re-designated JG 132 *'Richthofen'* display their new military markings. Warming up their engines at Jüterbog–Damm prior to take-off, these are aircraft of 6./JG 132, as witness the 'last two' of 'E-Emil' in the foreground – the '23' indicates, in reverse, the 3rd *Staffel* of the 2nd *Gruppe*

Also from II. *Gruppe*, these Heinkels have had their wheel spats removed in order to better cope with Jüterbog's sometimes less than ideal grass surface. Close scrutiny of the original print reveals that each aircraft carries an individual name (in small white letters on the red of the engine cowling immediately above the undercarriage leg fairing), that of the 4. *Staffel* machine on the left being *Greif* (Griffon). Note the camouflaged Ju 52/3m bomber-transport in the background

Taken during JG 132's brief flirtation with oversized fuselage codes (applied in an attempt to improve air-to-air recognition), this in-flight shot of 1. *Staffel's* 21+G11 also illustrates one of the pitfalls of black and white imagery. What, at first glance, appears to be an all-grey machine is, in fact, identical to those seen on the previous page – the tailband behind the white swastika disc, and the entire engine cowling and spinner, are painted bright *'Richthofen'* red

Major Johann Raithel was *Kommodore* of JG 132 for all of nine weeks before being elevated to the post of Inspector of Fighters. On 9 June Oberst Gerd von Massow was appointed to command the *Jagdgeschwader 'Richthofen'*.

The latter half of 1936 was spent in making good the losses in trained personnel which had been incurred by the *Gruppen's* involvement in establishing the four new fighter units earlier in the year. They were back to full strength and peak proficiency just in time for the second wave of planned expansions in the spring of 1937.

This latest programme called for the doubling of the existing number of *Jagdgruppen* from six to twelve, plus the subsequent creation of an additional twelve autonomous *Jagdstaffeln* – one to be set up by each individual *Jagdgruppe* – of which more later. In the event, only two of the six new *Gruppen* activated in the spring of 1937 were created around cadres drawn from Döberitz and Damm: I./JG 131, scheduled for deployment to Jesau in East Prussia, and II./JG 334, which was to be stationed at Mannheim.

The pruning of the *Geschwader's* strength early in 1937 was thus by no means as severe as that inflicted upon it the previous year. And any depletion it did suffer was more than compensated for in the weeks that followed when JG 132 was selected to be the first recipient of Professor Willy Messerschmitt's revolutionary new Bf 109 monoplane fighter.

After a brief transitional period spent testing the Bf 109B-0 pre-production version of this advanced aircraft under service conditions, the *Geschwader* (more precisely II./JG 132 at Jüterbog-Damm) had begun conversion on to the B-1, and later the B-2, production variants. By the end of the summer of 1937, JG 132's scarlet-nosed Heinkel biplanes had given way entirely to the sleek new machines, each one of which bore the

After Major Raithel's brief tenure of office, Oberstleutnant (later Oberst) Gerd von Massow would lead the *Geschwader* for almost four years

By September 1936 JG 132's unwieldy alpha-numeric fuselage codes had been replaced by a completely new system of high-visibility markings based upon white geometric symbols and individual aircraft numerals. This machine, combining the double chevron of a *Gruppenkommandeur* with the horizontal bar of II. *Gruppe*, thus proclaims itself to be the mount of Major Karl-August von Schönebeck

initial 'R', for Richthofen, in red script on a silver shield – the *Geschwader's* newly adopted badge – on its dark green fuselage.

The irrepressible II. *Gruppe* reportedly hit upon a novel method of celebrating their transition from the He 51 to the Messerschmitt by downing 109 bottles of beer! Whether their successors serving with the unit in its later wartime guise as I./NJG 1 were able to uphold such a splendid tradition, and double their alcohol intake, when they re-equipped with the Heinkel He 219 is unfortunately not on record!

In September 1937 large-scale manoeuvres involving all three branches of the Wehrmacht took place in northern Germany. JG 132's two Bf 109-equipped *Gruppen* provided the fighter backbone of 'Red force', and their performance – although marred by a spate of fatal accidents, which were later attributed to faulty stabiliser attachments – was followed with keen interest by the many foreign observers attending the exercises.

One notable omission from the 1937 war games was any form of nightfighter presence. While the greater part of the German military hierarchy fully supported Hitler's race to re-arm, there were the more cautious among their number who could foresee the dangers inherent in embarking upon an expansionist foreign policy backed up by displays of offensive force alone. Without a corresponding increase in her defences, Germany would be vulnerable to retaliatory attack. Both the British and French air forces possessed 'heavy' night-bombers (for example, the Handley Page Heyford and the Amiot 143M), and the best defence against the night-bomber, some argued, was the nightfighter.

Consequently, shortly after the end of the main 1937 manoeuvres a more limited and surreptitious series of night exercises were staged. These involved Arado Ar 68s flown by pilots of II./JG 132 in co-operation with the searchlights of Berlin. Although rudimentary in the extreme – single-seat biplanes operating from a grass field by the light of gooseneck flares was not exactly a quantum leap forward from the conditions which had existed at the close of World War 1 – these initial experiments obviously struck a chord with the authorities.

Further nightfighter trials would be carried out over the course of the next two years as tension in Europe mounted. In fact, the less reverent among the *'Richthofen'* pilots joked that they could always tell when the

The advent of the first Bf 109s in the spring of 1937 saw the introduction of the new *Geschwader* badge. Both these I. *Gruppe* B-2s, pictured later in the year, are sporting the red script 'R' on a silver shield below their windscreens

Führer was about to make another of his territorial demands – they would be up practising the nocturnal defence of his capital the week before!

In addition to developing their operational skills, JG 132 also continued in the role pioneered by the original *Fliegergruppe* Döberitz as the most favoured, and flaunted, of all Göring's fighter units. Throughout 1937 and into 1938 they played host to a constant stream of distinguished visitors.

Among the first of these had been a delegation of RAF officers headed by Air Vice-Marshal C L Courtney, Director of Operations and Intelligence. His six-day tour of the German aircraft industry and selected Luftwaffe airfields was made in January 1937, at a time when the *Geschwader* was still flying its colourful Heinkels. Later in the year came missions not only from Europe – Belgium, Poland and Sweden – but also from as far afield as South America and Japan.

When visited in January by the RAF's Air Vice-Marshal C L Courtney (accompanied here by the Reich's Secretary of State for Air Erhard Milch in white-lapelled General's uniform), I./JG 132 was still flying He 51s. Deep in conversation, the delegation completely ignores 2. *Staffel's* number '4'

Above
Another guest at Döberitz in early 1937 was Colonel Charles Lindbergh. Seen here in the civilian suit, the famous American aviator is displaying a much keener interest in these 1. *Staffel* Heinkels than the RAF officers featured on the previous page. In a return visit the following year, Lindbergh was given the opportunity to fly the Bf 109

Left
When Erhard Milch showed France's *Général* Joseph Vuillemin around Döberitz in August 1938, I. *Gruppe* was in the process of re-equipping with brand new Bf 109Cs. These modern fighters, and their smartly–overalled pilots, made a deep impression on the French Chief of Air Staff . . .

. . . who reported back to his government on the quality and modernity of Germany's growing air power

Nor did the flow of visiting dignitaries slacken in 1938, when three names stand out above all others: Marshal Balbo of Italy, *Général* Vuillemin, Chief of Staff of the French *Armée de l'Air* (who departed much chastened by the apparent might of the Luftwaffe – an impression helped along by some clever sleight of hand on the part of the conducting officers which entailed the *Général's* watching the same few aircraft taking off over and over again in seemingly unbroken succession!), and Col Charles Lindbergh, the famous American aviator and first man to fly solo across the Atlantic.

Lindbergh, too, was most impressed by a carefully conducted tour of the industry and a number of operational stations, during which he was permitted to fly the Bf 109. Believing the evidence of his own eyes and sincerely convinced of the Luftwaffe's superiority, Lindbergh returned to America to become a leading light in the Isolationist movement, later actively campaigning to keep the United States out of World War 2.

Despite the undoubted propaganda value of such visits from abroad, the *'Richthofen' Geschwader's* main responsibility remained, as before, the maintenance of a high level of operational readiness. Like any famous regiment of guards, they were not merely for display, but formed an integral part of their nation's armed forces. In the Germany of the late 1930s, this meant providing the muscle to back up their leader's demands on neighbouring territories and, in the unlikely event of an armed response, being prepared to defend their own airspace.

Not that there was much likelihood of retaliation in the face of the Führer's next 'foreign' venture: the annexation of Austria into the Greater German Reich. But the *Geschwader* did have a small part to play, with one *Staffel* of I./JG 132 transferring to Munich, and thence escorting Hitler's

But behind the scenes, and away from all the pomp and ceremony associated with visiting international dignitaries, Döberitz remained very much a working base. This section of perimeter track is a hive of activity (or is it the Luftwaffe equivalent of a NAAFI break?). Note the Gotha Go 145 'squadron hack' in the background, right, and the railway goods wagon on the single-line track in front of the hangar

The *Geschwader* was also learning to 'rough it' in the field – experience that would prove invaluable in the advance through France, now less than two years away

Ju 52 as he returned in triumph to the land of his birth. After four days at Wien-Aspern, the *Staffel* returned to Döberitz on 17 March.

The following month, on 21 April 1938 (the 20th anniversary of Manfred von Richthofen's death in action), Döberitz acted as host to its Commander-in-Chief when *Generalfeldmarschall* Göring unveiled a memorial stone to the fallen hero. Flanked during the ceremony by a red Fokker triplane on one side and a dark-green Bf 109 on the other, the stone was dedicated as a symbol of the bond between past and present.

With Austria safely under his belt, the Führer's attention now turned towards the largely German-speaking Sudeten territories of Czechoslovakia. Fully aware that he was unlikely to be greeted with the same open arms (at least by the Czech government) as had welcomed his troops' crossing of the Austrian border, Hitler ordered a build-up of his forces.

As part of this crash expansion programme the *Jagdgeschwader 'Richthofen'* suddenly found itself doubled in size. A III. *Gruppe* joined II./JG 132 at Jüterbog-Damm, while IV./JG 132 set up shop at Werneuchen, to the north-east of Berlin. Six other *Jagdgruppen* were also activated on this same 1 July 1938.

Only four of these eight simultaneous additions to the ranks of the *Jagdwaffe* were, in fact, completely new units. The remainder – and this included III./JG 132 – had been made up from those 12 additional *Staffeln* established independently in the early summer of 1937, and now hastily re-organised into *Gruppen*.

With Messerschmitt's production lines already stretched to peak capacity, it was impossible to equip this mass influx in its entirety with Bf 109s. The majority of the newcomers had perforce to fly obsolescent Arado and Heinkel biplanes.

The component *Staffeln* of Major D.-Ing. Bormann's III./JG 132, for example, retained the elderly Ar 68s with which they had been operating on an autonomous basis for the past year. Theo Osterkamp's IV./JG 132, on the other hand, having been formed from scratch around a nucleus of instructors and graduates from Werneuchen's resident flying school's advanced fighter courses, were more fortunate in being equipped with a number of that establishment's Bf 109 trainers.

One report suggests that IV./JG 132 received further reinforcements in the shape of a dozen Heinkel He 112B-0 fighters currently being readied for export to Japan. It is claimed by some that the Heinkels (a design which had lost out to the Bf 109 for acceptance as the Luftwaffe's standard fighter) were flown by one *Staffel* of IV./JG 132 during the period of the Sudeten crisis. Others dispute this fact, maintaining that photographs of the He 112 in Luftwaffe service markings – like those of the infamous 'He 113' of the early months of the war – were pure propaganda, released to 'confound and confuse the enemy'.

A more definite indication of the growing seriousness of the Sudeten situation was the re-establishment of the experimental nightfighter unit Döberitz in September. Commanded by Oberleutnant Blumensaat, an ex-gunnery instructor at Lipetsk and now a dedicated advocate of the nightfighter, this *Staffel*-strong formation of Ar 68s was even accorded an official designation – 10.(N)/JG 132.

If the nocturnal defence of the capital was exercising the minds of those in power, the Czechoslovakian crisis was obviously approaching its climax. But the quantity, if not the uniform quality, of the forces backing the Führer's latest demands were to prove more than sufficient against a Western coalition with both feet already firmly planted on the slippery slope of appeasement.

At half-past midnight on the morning of 30 September 1938, Hitler, Mussolini, Chamberlain and Daladier signed the Munich Agreement, ceding the Czech Sudeten territories to Germany. On the following day German troops, supported by some 500 aircraft, marched unopposed across the frontier. And ten days after that it was announced that the Luftwaffe had taken possession of all Czech airfields and installations within the agreed zone of occupation.

On 11 November 1938 far-reaching changes were to be introduced throughout the *Jagdwaffe*. This was the date on which a distinction was first drawn between *leichte* (light) and *schwere* (heavy) *Jagdgruppen*. The latter – fore-runners of the war-time *Zerstörergruppen* – would now be identifiable by the number '4' as the middle digit of their three-figure unit designation.

Two of the *Jagdgeschwader 'Richthofen's'* four *Gruppen* were affected by this division – the long-standing II./JG 132, commanded now by Major

A mystery still to be solved. Did IV./JG 132 really operate a *Staffel* of Heinkel He 112B-0s at the time of the Munich crisis, or were these machines – destined for export to Japan – painted in Luftwaffe markings purely as a propaganda ploy?

Although it has been suggested in the past that these anonymous, fully camouflaged Ar 68Es are machines of Oberleutnant Blumensaat's nightfighting 10. *Staffel*, proof positive is still lacking

Joachim-Friedrich Huth, would remain at Jüterbog-Damm, but under the new identity of I./JG 141, while the relative newcomers of III./JG 132, having been transferred in the meantime from Jüterbog to Fürstenwalde, were transformed into II./JG 141.

At the same time as these two *Gruppen* joined the newly-formed ranks of the 'heavy fighters' (later to metamorphose into I./ZG 1 and I./ZG 76 respectively), Theo Osterkamp's IV./JG 132 was redesignated I./JG 331 (the later I./JG 77). This unit's recent perambulations had taken it from Werneuchen to Leipzig – its jumping-off point for the Sudeten operation – to Karlsbad, just across the now defunct border, and thence to Mährisch-Trübau (Moravská Trebová, an ex-Czech airfield deep in Moravia).

These changes meant that Oberstleutnant von Massow suddenly had but a single *Gruppe* left to his name as titular *Kommodore* of the Reich's premier fighter unit. And, to complicate matters still further, von Massow's command was now known officially as JG 131 *'Richthofen'*. This alteration to the last digit of the three-figure designator was brought about by the six former territorial *Luftkreiskommandos* of 1934 vintage being replaced by just three larger *Luftwaffengruppenkommandos*. Units such as the *Jagdgeschwader 'Richthofen'*, which were based in the Berlin area, and originally part of *Luftkreis II*, now came under the control of Lw.Gr.Kdo. 1. Although the organisational change had come into effect on 4 February, the intervening Sudeten crisis had delayed redesignations at unit level until 11 November 1938.

During the ensuing winter months the *Geschwaderstab* and I./JG 131 'Richthofen', both still at Döberitz, converted fully to the Bf 109C. And in mid-January 1939, Oberleutnant Blumensaat's nightfighter *Staffel* of

The only authenticated picture of a 10.(N)/JG 131 machine is this tantalising glimpse of the starboard wingtips of one of Blumensaat's biplanes. Again, fuller details are wanting, but the *Staffel* bus and camouflage netting would seem to suggest a temporary deployment, while the 'WL'-code on the Klemm Kl 35 communications aircraft in the background dates it somewhere between January and October 1939

On 21 April 1939, the 21st anniversary of the death of Manfred von Richthofen, a wreath-laying ceremony was held at the memorial stone which had been unveiled at Döberitz the year before. Visible in front of the stone on this occasion are Gerd von Massow (in helmet), Hermann Göring and the mother and brother of the fallen hero. The diagonal white line above Göring's head is the propeller of one of the *Geschwader's* Bf 109s

Ar 68s was once again revived, this time as 10.(N)/JG 131. Its resurrection could mean only one thing – the Führer was once more bent on redrawing the map of Europe.

Sure enough, early in March I./JG 131 found itself heading south to take part in the second and final act of Hitler's clinical dismemberment of Czechoslovakia. On 15 March, despite local blizzards, the German army occupied the remainder of the Czech states of Bohemia and Moravia. The following day these territories were formally annexed as a protectorate, joining the Sudetenland within the borders of the Greater German Reich.

Once again the Luftwaffe, poised on nearby airfields to strike at the first signs of serious resistance, found that its services were not needed. But by 17 March the weather had at least cleared sufficiently to permit its participation in the victory celebrations organised in the former Czech capital. Some 400 aircraft, including the Bf 109s of I./JG 131, flew in from their temporary base at Karlsbad. They roared in serried ranks low over ancient Prague's Hradcany Castle in an impressive display of Germany's growing military might.

Shortly thereafter the *Gruppe* returned to Döberitz for re-equipment with the latest Bf 109E variant. And it was here, on 1 May 1939, and upon the introduction of a greatly simplified 'block' system of unit designation (the block system allocated numbers 1-25 to units serving under *Luftflotte 1*, 26-50 to *Luftflotte 2*, 51-75 to *Luftflotte 3* and 76-99 to *Luftflotte 4)*, that they finally emerged as *Jagdgeschwader* 2 *'Richthofen'*.

Just why numerical pride of place within this new system went to I./JG 1, a solitary *Gruppe* in far-off East Prussia, is not quite clear. But it was as JG 2 that the Luftwaffe's senior most fighter unit would embark upon, and fight throughout, World War 2.

With war rapidly approaching, no chances were being taken. I./JG 2's new Bf 109E-1s are kept carefully hidden from prying eyes, be they on the ground or in the air

HOSTILITIES

When the Luftwaffe opened the hostilities against Poland shortly after 0430 hrs on the morning of 1 September 1939, JG 2's serviceable strength of 52 Bf 109s was just one short of full establishment. It comprised the three Bf 109Es of Oberstleutnant von Massow's own *Geschwaderstabskette*, 40 (out of 41) Bf 109Es of Major Vieck's I. *Gruppe* and nine Bf 109Ds (which had replaced the earlier Ar 68s) of Hauptmann Blumensaat's 10.(N)/JG 2.

But the *Jagdgeschwader 'Richthofen'* was to play only a very minor part in the subjugation of Poland. Its main task was the aerial defence of the German capital. To this end, and fearing retaliatory nocturnal strikes by the small, but efficient, Polish air force, Blumensaat's nightfighters had been transferred to Strausberg, some 12 miles (20 km) to the east of Berlin. Detachments of I./JG 2 from Döberitz also used Strausberg as a forward base.

These precautions seemed fully justified on the very first evening of the war, when the capital's sirens wailed into life at 1831 hours. Almost the whole of JG 2 was scrambled to meet the threat, only to discover that the 'attackers' were Heinkel bombers returning from a raid on Warsaw airport.

Britain and France's declaration of war on Germany less than 48 hours later meant that Berlin now faced possible danger from the west too. Elements of JG 2 were therefore despatched to Brandenburg, about 22 miles (35 km) beyond the city's western suburbs. But not a single enemy bomber approached the capital of the Third Reich, either from east or west, by day or night.

1 September 1939. Men of the signals section gather round a civilian radio set to hear the Führer announce the outbreak of hostilities against Poland

For the first few weeks of the war Hauptmann Blumensaat's Bf 109D nightfighters stood ready to defend Berlin against nocturnal attack. But none was forthcoming

The continuing dearth of aerial activity above their own heads presumably persuaded the powers-that-be to release a *Staffel* of I./JG 2 for operations against the Poles. Accordingly, 1. *Staffel* flew into Prostken, situated right on East Prussia's border with Poland, on 9 September. But by this stage of the campaign Polish skies were as empty as those over Berlin. The pilots of 1./JG 2 failed to encounter a single hostile aircraft during their short sojourn in the east. Having to be content with a few ground-strafing missions, principally against road and rail targets, the *Staffel* returned to Döberitz on 15 September.

Indeed, it was over the Greater Berlin area that the *Jagdgeschwader 'Richthofen'* reportedly suffered its first casualties of the war. One source indicates that two aircraft crashed on the night of 16-17 September – one a Bf 109 of I./JG 2, and the other an Ar 68 of 10. *Staffel* (the latter suggesting that, although officially equipped with Bf 109Ds, 10.(N)/JG 2 still retained at least some of its elderly biplanes on strength). The two pilots were killed.

According to the findings of a subsequent enquiry, the likeliest cause was that both had been blinded by the reflective glare of the capital's searchlights. But the loss of a 10. *Staffel* Bf 109D to 'friendly' flak over the city's northern outskirts the following month (the pilot on this occasion fortunately being able to bail out unhurt) points to another possible explanation.

Before the end of September Karl Vieck, the long-serving *Kommandeur* of I./JG 2, was promoted to Oberst and departed Döberitz to take command of JG 3. His replacement was Hauptmann Jürgen Roth, one of the original *Staffelführer* of the *Legion Condor's* fighter force in Spain. Little over a month later it was the turn of I./JG 2 to bid farewell to the base which had been the unit's home since its activation as *Fliegergruppe* Döberitz over five-and-a-half years before.

Early in November 1939 – with the campaign in Poland long over, the Reich's eastern frontiers secured by a treaty with the Soviet Union, and her capital yet to see an enemy bomber – *Stab* and I./JG 2 were transferred from Berlin to take their place along the *Westwall* as part of the build-up of German forces facing the French.

Moves were now in hand to bring the *Jagdgeschwader 'Richthofen'* up to full three-*Gruppe* complement, but as it would be several weeks before the new units were declared operational, Oberst von Massow was temporarily assigned two other *Gruppen*. I./JG 77 was already stationed at Frankfurt's Rhein-Main airfield when I./JG 2 flew in to neighbouring Rebstock. Within days, however, the former had decamped to Cologne. They were replaced at Rhein-Main by I./JG 76 – another ex-metropolitan defence *Gruppe* recently arrived in the west from Vienna.

The *Geschwader's* new area of operations was centred along the Saarland region of the German border to the south of neutral Luxembourg. Prohibited from violating the Duchy's airspace, each side made extensive use of the Saarland 'corridor' as a means of access to the other's territory. During these early months – the period of the so-called 'Phoney War' – such overflights were almost exclusively for purposes of reconnaissance. JG 2's tasks were twofold – to fly defensive patrols in order to deter any inquisitive Frenchman from probing too deeply into Germany's frontier fortifications, and to escort the Luftwaffe's own reconnaissance machines during their forays over France.

A pensive Leutnant Helmut Wick of 3./JG 2. He scored the *Geschwader's* first kill – a French Curtiss Hawk H-75 – over the western front on 22 November 1939

It was during one such reconnaissance mission that the *Jagdgeschwader 'Richthofen'* achieved its first two victories of World War 2. 3./JG 2's orders for that morning of 22 November 1939 did not require them to provide close escort. Instead, they were to mount *freie Jagd* (free hunting) sweeps ahead of the reconnaissance Dornier to clear its planned flightpath of any aerial opposition (see *Osprey Aircraft of the Aces 11 - Bf 109D/E Aces 1939-41* for further details).

One of the pilots assigned to fly this routine sortie was a relatively unknown and unsung young leutnant named Helmut Wick. The French Curtiss Hawk H-75A of GC II/4 which Wick despatched over Phalsbourg, north-west of Strasbourg, shortly after midday did more than simply open the *Geschwader's* scoreboard – it also marked the start of a personal combat career which was little short of meteoric.

Within the space of a year, the obscure leutnant would rise from the position of *Rottenführer* (leader of a two-aircraft section) in 3. *Staffel* to *Geschwaderkommodore* of JG 2 *'Richthofen'* – a feat which remained unparalleled in the history of the Luftwaffe – and emerge as Germany's then highest-scoring fighter ace in the process.

Later lauded as a national hero in print and on newsreel, Helmut Wick penned his own 'factual' account of the 22 November mission for the Luftwaffe magazine *Der Adler*;

'As the French did not cross the German border very often, my wingman and I decided for once to visit them. A tail-wind from the east helped us on our way.

'Near Nancy I suddenly saw a gaggle of aircraft at an altitude of some 6000 metres (9850 ft). Realising at once that they were not German, we began to circle. Two machines detached themselves from the bunch above and swooped down on us. Now I could make out what they were: Curtiss fighters.

'We dived away and, just as we had anticipated, the two Frenchmen dived after us. I pulled into a climbing turn with one of the Frenchmen right on my tail. I can still clearly recall his red, white and blue roundels as I looked behind me. At first, the sight of them was rather exciting, especially as the Frenchman was blazing away with all barrels. But then the realisation that somebody is on your tail and shooting at you becomes very unpleasant.

'I pushed the nose down again and, with my superior speed, quickly lost him. When my Frenchman was no longer to be seen, I looked up to my left to find the others. Not a thing in sight. I glanced up to the right and could scarcely believe my eyes. I was staring straight at four radial engines, all spitting little red flames. A ridiculous thought flashed through my mind – "Are they really allowed to shoot at me like that?"

'But then I was all concentration. Should I try to get away again? No! Now's the time to tackle them. One of them has got to go down. Clenching my teeth, I hauled the stick and rudder to the right and turned into them.

'By the time I had completed my turn the leader had already overshot me. The second was right behind him, and this one I attacked head-on. It was a nasty moment staring straight down his blazing gun barrels, but we were too close to each other to score any hits. He flashed past over my head and now the third one was almost on top of me.

'I manoeuvred my aircraft slightly to get this one nicely lined up in my sights, aiming and firing exactly as I had been taught at fighter training school. With my first shots I saw some pieces of metal fly off the Frenchman. Then both his wings buckled and gave way.

'Close behind him the fourth Curtiss was also shooting at me. But I was not hit. The first pair were now climbing again. I followed suit so that they could not catch me. My fuel was running low and it was time to head for home. My wingman, who had returned to base safe and sound, had lost me after the first dive in all the twisting and turning.'

Wick's wingman during JG 2's first successful engagement was Oberfeldwebel Erwin Kley, who also accounted for a Hawk H-75 in the same engagement. Here, he points to his second victory (yet another Hawk, this time shot down near Charleville on 15 May 1940). After claiming the *Geschwader's* first B-17, 'Icke' Kley would be killed on 19 August 1942 – the day of the abortive Canadian landings at Dieppe

Christmas 1939 at Frankfurt-Rebstock. By the time II./JG 2 was activated in the winter of 1939-40, the previously dark-green camouflage of the *Emils* had given way to a more suitable paler finish. Pilots of 3./JG 2 peer out of the 'Café Archambault' – the *Staffel's* readiness hut. Both Ofw Franz Jänisch (front left in window) and Lt Rudolf Pflanz (extreme right in window) would claim their first kills during the remaining weeks of the 'phoney war'

In fact, Oberfeldwebel Erwin Kley had claimed another of GC II/4's Hawks at also the same moment as Wick's victim went down.

Wick then concluded his account by admitting that the action had very nearly not taken place at all. Just before take-off his aircraft had been washed down, and during the climb to altitude on the outward flight a film of ice had begun to form on the Messerschmitt. He had seriously considered aborting the mission. These freezing conditions, which were to blanket the whole of the western front in thick snow, heralded the onset of one of the region's worst winters for decades. Flying was to be severely impeded for the best part of three months, and it would be March 1940 before I./JG 2 claimed its next kill.

Although winter was tightening its grip, the expansion of Luftwaffe forces continued apace. The *'Richthofen' Geschwader's* new II. *Gruppe*, which had been forming at Zerbst, was declared operational in December. It was commanded by Hauptmann Wolfgang Schellmann who, like I./JG 2's Jürgen Roth, was a veteran of the Spanish Civil War (with 12 Republican kills to his credit, Schellmann was one of the *Legion Condor's* most successful fighter pilots, second only to the legendary Werner Mölders).

The snow still lay thick on the ground at Frankfurt in mid-March 1940. Are 'Icke' Kley's ears cold, or is somebody 'gunning' that *Emil's* engine a little too noisily? Leutnant Franz Fiby (centre) seems more amused than deafened, while Franz Jänisch remains totally unconcerned

***Staffelkapitän* of 3./JG 2 at Frankfurt was Hauptmann Hennig Strümpell (second left). Behind him (left to right) are Franz Jänisch, the tall figure of Olt Jobst Hauenschild – who would be credited with JG 2's only victory on the opening day of the *Blitzkrieg* in the west – and Feldwebel Edmund Wagner. The latter left the *Geschwader* before the end of 1940 to join JG 51, and would be awarded a posthumous Knight's Cross in November 1941**

II./JG 2 did not immediately join the *Geschwader* on the western front, however. It remained in central Germany for the first three months, reportedly guarding vital industrial targets in the region, before being transferred to Nordholz to bolster the defences of the North Sea coast, and its major ports, in mid-March 1940.

By that time JG 2 had been brought up to full establishment by the creation of a III. *Gruppe*. The order for this unit's activation at Vienna-Schwechat had been given back in October, but it was not until the end of February 1940 that III./JG 2 became fully operational. It, too, was initially retained in central Germany, being based at Magdeburg under the command of 41-year-old Major Dr Erich Mix, a World War 1 pilot who had claimed three victories in that earlier conflict.

For a brief period the *Jagdgeschwader 'Richthofen'* even equalled its peak pre-Sudeten strength of four *Gruppen*. The wartime IV. *Gruppe* never operated as an integral part of the parent unit, however, and its association with JG 2 was little more than administrative.

It originated with Hauptmann Blumensaat's *Staffel* of nightfighters. During the opening weeks of the war 10.(N)/JG 2 had continued zealously to guard Berlin throughout the hours of darkness (latterly, it is reported, with the cockpit roof glazing of their Bf 109Ds removed to reduce reflected searchlight glare – a lesson learned from the night of 16-17 September, perhaps?).

But the equally steadfast refusal on the part of the Allies to bomb Germany's cities by night persuaded the RLM that the *Staffel* could be more usefully employed elsewhere. It also convinced them that there was no necessity to add further to the Luftwaffe's meagre nightfighter arm. They did decide, however, that the three hitherto autonomous *Nachtstaffeln* which made up this force should be combined to form a single entity.

As a consequence, 10.(N)/JG 26 and 11.(N)/LG 2 joined with 10.(N)/JG 2 in February 1940 to become IV.(N)/JG 2. Command was entrusted to the experienced Hauptmann Blumensaat. Having thus created the new *Gruppe*, its component *Staffeln* were promptly dispersed about the north German seaboard – Blumensaat's *Gruppenstab* and 11. *Staffel* (ex-11.(N)/LG 2) were based at Jever, the original 10.(N)/JG 2 out on Langeoog, one of the offshore Frisian Islands, and 12.(N)/JG 2 (the ex-10.(N)/JG 26) at Lüneburg. This last *Staffel* subsequently transferred to Marx, while the *Gruppe* also temporarily deployed a small *Kommando* at Rostock, on the Baltic coast.

But it was not over these northern waters that IV.(N)/JG 2 was to achieve its first success. By the spring of 1940 the *Gruppe* had been ordered to redeploy several small detachments inland. On the night of 20-21 April – nearly eight months after the outbreak of hostilities – Oberfeldwebel Willi Schmale finally scored the Luftwaffe's first nightfighter kill of World War 2. He brought down a Fairy Battle I of No 218 Sqn, part of the RAF's AASF (Advanced Air Striking Force) based in France, which had been busily engaged in 'Nickelling' (leaflet-dropping) near Crailsheim, north-east of Stuttgart.

Of the three-man crew of Battle P2201, only the pilot survived – and his one-man war against the Germans was far from over. Canadian Plt Off H D 'Hank' Wardle subsequently became a prisoner in, and successful escapee from, the notorious *Oflag* IVC PoW camp, now better known simply as Colditz.

Five nights later it was the turn of one of the coastal pilots to claim the *Gruppe's* second victory. Oberfeldwebel Hermann Förster's victim, believed to be Hampden I P1319 of No 49 Sqn, which he shot into the sea off the southern tip of the island of Sylt, was the first aircraft of the RAF's UK-based Bomber Command to be lost to a Luftwaffe nightfighter.

The *Emil* of *Geschwaderkommodore* Oberst Gerd von Massow is seen at Frankfurt shortly before his elevation to the post of *Jagdführer 3*

Although technically nightfighters, the *Doras* of Hauptmann Blumensaat's IV.(N)/JG 2 wore a predominantly hellblau finish similar to that used by the rest of the *Geschwader's* Bf 109s. These are machines of 11. *Staffel*, and they are seen at Trondheim-Vaernes during the *Gruppe's* brief deployment to Norway in early May

By this time the German invasion of Norway was nearing its conclusion, and the *Blitzkrieg* in the west, against France and the Low Countries, was about to be launched. Neither campaign brought any success to IV.(N)/JG 2, which was peripherally involved in both. But the escalation of the night bombing offensive against Germany, mounted in response to Hitler's assault in the west, soon prompted the Luftwaffe to alter its stance on the creation of a nocturnal fighter defence force.

And while the core of the new nightfighter arm would be provided by redesignating and retraining many of the twin-engined *Zerstörergruppen*, it was only natural that IV.(N)/JG 2 – the only unit with practical night-fighting experience – should join its ranks. On 22 June 1940 the *Gruppe* was officially redesignated II./NJG 1 (only to undergo a second change of identity nine days later when it became III./NJG 1). This effectively severed its last tenuous links with JG 2 *'Richthofen'*.

But let us now return to the period of the 'Phoney War' and the *Geschwader* proper. A slight easing of the wintry conditions had led to a resumption of the sporadic sparring between the opposing fighter forces stationed along the western front. On the afternoon of 9 March JG 2 scored its third victory when seven aircraft of 3. *Staffel* clashed with twice that number of Morane MS.406s of GC II/5 close to the Saarland border. Oberfeldwebel Franz Jänisch claimed hits on one of the French fighters, which was written-off when its wounded pilot attempted a crash-landing back at Metz.

April opened with the promotion of Oberst Gerd von Massow to the post of *Jafü* 3. The new *Kommodore* of the *Jagdgeschwader 'Richthofen'* was Oberst Harry von Bülow-Bothkamp, a six-victory World War 1 ace, one-time *Staffelführer* of the famed *Jasta Boelcke*, and more recently *Gruppenkommandeur* of II./JG 77.

The month of April also saw three more kills added to the *Geschwader's* scoreboard, with two pilots of 1. *Staffel* claiming victories on consecutive days. On the 20th Oberleutnant Otto Bertram shot down a Hawk H-75A – part of the fighter escort for a reconnaissance Potez – in the Saarbrücken area, although this encounter cost 1./JG 2 two aircraft damaged, with one of the pilots being wounded.

Von Massow's successor was Oberstleutnant (later Oberst) Harry von Bülow-Bothkamp. He would lead the *Geschwader* throughout the Battle of France and into the Battle of Britain

In the final few weeks leading up to the invasion of France I./JG 2 transferred from Frankfurt to Bassenheim, in the Eifel foothills west of Koblenz. Presumably just returned from a routine patrol, Leutnant Helmut Wick and Unteroffizier Günther Seeger are about to be greeted by a rather shaggy dog!

The following day the price was even higher, for while Oberleutnant Karl-Heinz Krahl was able to claim the destruction of a MS.406, two other *Schwärme* (sections of four aircraft) of 1. *Staffel* were engaged by AASF Hurricanes of No 73 Sqn. This latter action, which took place south-west of Trier, resulted in the *Geschwader's* first combat fatality of the war. Although Oberfeldwebel Werner Höppner was seen to bail out of his stricken Messerschmitt, he had been mortally wounded, and died before rescuers could reach him.

On the last day of April over the same area south of the so-called *Dreiländereck* (literally 'three nations corner' – the point where the Franco-German frontier touches the southern tip of Luxembourg), Leutnant Rudolf Pflanz of 3./JG 2 was instrumental in bringing down a French Potez 63. But as Helmut Wick and Jobst Hauenschild also had a hand in the destruction of the reconnaissance twin, it was officially credited as a joint *Staffel* victory.

During the final weeks leading up to the launch of the *Blitzkrieg* in the west, the *Gruppen* of JG 2 had been redeployed from Frankfurt to more forward landing grounds closer to their forthcoming area of operations. For the *Geschwaderstab* and I./JG 2 this meant a move up to the line of the River Moselle to Wengerohr and Bassenheim, respectively. III. *Gruppe*, which had been transferred from Magdeburg to Frankfurt earlier in April, now took up residence at Freschweiler, close to the German-Luxembourg border.

III. *Gruppe's* jumping-off point for the *Blitzkrieg* in the west was Freschweiler, close to the Luxembourg border. Here, 'White 2' of 7. *Staffel* is being refuelled ready for the next sortie

To make up his numbers, Oberst von Bülow-Bothkamp retained control of the attached I./JG 76, for II./JG 2 had still not yet joined the main body of the *Geschwader*. While the latter formed part of *Luftflotte* 3's strength on the southern flank of the invasion front, Hauptmann Schellmann's II. *Gruppe*, having moved in the meantime from Nordholz to Münster, would operate during the opening stages of the coming campaign as a component of the reinforced JG 26 under *Luftflotte 2* in the northern sector.

Thus, the stage was set for the advance into France – the country that was to be the *'Richthofen' Geschwader's* home for the next four years.

BLITZKRIEG IN THE WEST

In the early hours of 10 May 1940, waves of paratroop-laden and glider-tug Ju 52/3m tri-motor transports crossed the Dutch and Belgian frontiers. Their occupants formed the spearheads of Army Group B's northern flank assault. This right-hand pincer of the *Blitzkrieg* against the western allies had a two-fold objective.

Not only was it intended to breach the Low Countries' immediate border defences, it was also designed to draw the British Expeditionary Force (BEF) out of the fortified positions it had been constructing in eastern France throughout the winter. By moving forward to the aid of Belgium, the BEF would be leaving in its wake a dangerously thinly-held gap between itself and the main bulk of the French army still ensconced behind the Maginot Line.

As part of the fighter forces assigned to cover this northern offensive, II./JG 2 (under the temporary control of JG 26) carried out a number of transport- and bomber-escort duties over Holland on the first day of the campaign. But it was on 11 May, after they transferred from Münster to a more forward landing ground at Hamminkeln, closer to the Dutch border, that *Kommandeur* Hauptmann Schellmann opened the *Gruppe's* scoreboard by claiming a Hurricane near Couly.

Thereafter, II./JG 2 followed in the footsteps of the ground troops as they advanced through Belgium. 14 May saw them touch down for the

On temporary secondment to JG 26, the Bf 109s of II./JG 2 were halfway through their advance across Belgium when this picture of 'White 12' was taken at Tirlemont in mid-May. Note the pile of equipment outside the tent and the stacked rifles. The somewhat underdressed figure between the two is the otherwise always sartorially immaculate Hans 'Assi' Hahn

first time on occupied soil at Peer, and 72 hours later they made the 31-mile (50-km) hop to Tirlemont, east of Brussels. Here they stayed just over a week, before moving on to Grandglise (Quevaucamps), hard by the French frontier, on 25 May.

Throughout this period the *Gruppe* added a further 18 RAF kills (the majority of them Hurricanes), plus one errant Frenchman, to its communal total. A number of personalities later to figure prominently in the history of JG 2 achieved their first successes over Belgium at this time.

On the morning of 14 May, while escorting a formation of Hs 123 ground-attack biplanes against targets in the Louvain area, the *Staffelkapitän* of 4./JG 2 – a certain Leutnant Hans Hahn – claimed two Hurricanes of No 607 Sqn. A third fell to Feldwebel Karl-Heinz Harbauer, whilst another of Hahn's NCO pilots, one Oberfeldwebel Siegfried Schnell, was responsible for the *Gruppe's* sole French victim – reportedly a Bloch 152.

4. *Staffel* was again in the forefront of the action five days later. This time its pilots were flying escort for He 111 bombers when, shortly after midday on 19 May, Hans Hahn – promoted in the interim to Oberleutnant – and Leutnant Julius Meimberg each downed a Hurricane.

But, perhaps not surprisingly, the lion's share of the *Gruppe's* kills went to its experienced *Kommandeur*. Wolfgang Schellmann had already added a brace each of Hurricanes and Lysanders to his earlier dozen *Legion Condor* victories when he closed II./JG 2's account against the RAF in this first stage of the *Blitzkrieg* in the west by downing three more British machines on three successive days – a Spitfire on 31 May, a Lysander on 1 June and another Spitfire 24 hours later – all in the Dunkirk area.

For by now the BEF's ill-starred advance into Belgium had ended in defeat and the ignominy of the evacuation. Although several pilots had been wounded, II./JG 2's sole combat fatality in the 25-day campaign was Leutnant Wilhelm Schetelig of 5. *Staffel*, who had failed to return from a sortie on 27 May.

The route II./JG 2 had just taken through Belgium was an historic one, for it followed the path of the famous 'Schlieffen Plan' – the powerful right hook with which the Kaiser's army had launched its offensive against the west in 1914. The Anglo-French High Command assumed at first that Hitler was about to repeat the same tactic in this present conflict.

But two new factors had been added to the equation of offensive warfare since the outbreak of World War 1 – air power and armoured mobility. The Führer's main thrust would come from an entirely unexpected quarter. Although dramatically successful in its own right, Army Group B's northern advance was also a gigantic feint. The real blow would be delivered by the Panzers of von Rundstedt's Army Group A, debouching from the 'impenetrable' forests of the Ardennes to the south, and making use of the gap opened up by the BEF's advance into Belgium to dash headlong for the Channel coast, thereby splitting Anglo-French forces in two.

The cutting edge of Army Group A was made up of the five armoured divisions of the *Panzergruppe von Kleist*. Their aerial support would be provided by the fighters of *Luftflotte 3*, which included *Stab*, I. and III./JG 2 (plus the attached I./JG 76).

At 0530 hours on 10 May, while the world's attention was focused on Germany's airborne invasion of the Low Countries, 1. *Panzerdivision*

In the two weeks following the 'Day of the Fighters', JG 2 claimed over 100 victories, with many famous names opening their scoring during this period. The unidentified pilot flying 3. *Staffel's* 'Yellow 9' already has four kill bars adorning his tailfin. Could this be the same 'Yellow 9', named *Motti*, which was parked beside the 'Café Archambault' (on page 28) at Christmas?

slipped almost unnoticed into Luxembourg. By that same evening it was across the Duchy and through the frontier defences of Belgium. Allied resistance, confined in the main to units of French cavalry and cyclists of the Belgian *Chasseurs Ardennais*, was swept aside. Forty-eight hours later the leading Panzers reached the banks of the River Meuse – the one major obstacle which could thwart their drive to the Channel. Supported by Stukas, they began crossing it the following day.

Up until this point von Kleist's Panzer divisions, well hidden among the tree-covered slopes and deep-shadowed valleys of the Ardennes, had not been subject to serious Allied air attack. The local French commander appeared more puzzled than perturbed at the enemy activity on his front. Indeed, JG 2's only kill during the first four days of the advance was an inquisitive Potez 63 reconnaissance twin brought down by Oberleutnant Jobst Hauenschild of 3. *Staffel*. But all this was to change on 14 May.

Suddenly aware of the magnitude of the disaster which was threatening to engulf them, Allied chiefs ordered everything that could fly to target the Meuse bridgeheads near Sedan. All day long, in a series of largely uncoordinated penny-packet attacks, Allied bombers sought to knock out the pontoon bridges spanning the river.

In the early morning ten single-engined Fairy Battles of the RAF tried and failed. Shortly after midday a dozen lumbering, slab-sided Amiot 143 night-bombers of the *Armée de l'Air* were equally unsuccessful. They were followed by more French medium and assault bombers. In the late afternoon the entire remaining bomber strength of the RAF's AASF – some 71 Battles and Blenheims in all – made one last attempt.

The sporadic nature of the these attacks, and the sometimes lengthy intervals between them, meant that each was faced with a freshly armed and refuelled force of defending Luftwaffe fighters waiting to intercept it. Despite the best efforts of the bombers' own escorting fighters, the result was carnage. By the end of the day – which became known in the Luftwaffe as the 'Day of the Fighters' – no fewer than 89 Allied aircraft had been shot down.

This busy panoramic view shows one of the landing grounds – possibly near Charleville – that was occupied by III./JG 2 as it leapfrogged through France in the wake of the advancing Panzers. With aircraft and vehicles casually dispersed across the open ground, little more than lip service is being paid to the threat of Allied air attack. Camouflage is rudimentary in the extreme (note the branches placed against the noses of the two *Emils* on the horizon), and the only sign of anti-aircraft defence is the single machine-gun mounted on the Kfz 12 Adler car on the left

Close on half this total was claimed by JG 53, the famous 'Ace-of-Spades' unit. But the two *Gruppen* of the *Jagdgeschwader 'Richthofen'* had between them accounted for 16 enemy aircraft destroyed. And just as II./JG 2's current campaign across Belgium was providing the opportunity for a number of well-known names of the future to open their scoring, so the 'Day of the Fighters' along the Meuse also gave several of the *Geschwader's* subsequent Knight's Cross winners their first step up on the ladder of fame.

2. *Staffel's* Feldwebel Erich Rudorffer, for example, claimed a Hawk H-75 during one of the mid-afternoon French raids, and Leutnant Erich Leie of III. *Gruppe* downed an RAF Blenheim some seven miles (12 km) east of Sedan at 1920 hours. One of the last units aloft that day was 1./JG 2, whose Oberfeldwebel Werner Machold was credited with a pair of MS.406s shortly after 2000 hours.

After the hectic activity of 14 May, the following day proved relatively quiet. I./JG 2's sole victory was another reconnaissance Potez, as recounted by the *Gruppenstab's* Leutnant Paul Temme;

'I was on patrol with the *Kommandeur* (Hauptmann Roth) in the Sedan region. We were being escorted by four aircraft of 1. *Staffel.* A solitary army co-op machine was circling south of Sedan – probably counting trucks on the road below. Flying between the cumulus – sometimes above, sometimes below – we lost our escort.

'We were some 300 metres (1000 ft) below the clouds when a twin-engined machine appeared out of the cloud base heading straight towards us. I recognised it as a French Potez. It obviously spotted us as it passed overhead. But instead of disappearing straight back up into the clouds again, it tried to get away by banking to the right.

'The *Kommandeur* turned after it, but on the wrong side. I banked in the opposite direction and immediately found the Frenchman square in my sights. I eased a little closer. The rear gunner opened fire at me.

'I pressed the firing button and kept my finger on it as I moved in closer still. The rear gunner had stopped shooting. The enemy banked left, then right. I sent a burst into his fuselage and the cockpit roof flew off. A figure struggled to emerge, appeared to be caught by one leg for a few seconds, but then fell free. His parachute blossomed below me.

'The Potez was now flying straight and level. There was no movement from the cockpit. I drew up alongside and had a closer look. Two figures hunched at front and back. It was the middle one who had bailed out. So back on its tail to give it another burst.

'The undercarriage dropped. The machine nosed into a steep dive towards the woods below. I followed it down. It went into the trees, snapping them off like match sticks. Then impact and a ball of fire. I circled the spot and got a "Bravo" from the *Kommandeur* over my headphones. My first kill!'

Once safely across the Meuse, the leading Panzers gathered pace, biting daily ever deeper into the French rear. JG 2 had already moved forward from its jumping off points along the Moselle to Bastogne, in Belgium. But within 48 hours, in order to keep up with the rapid advance of the ground forces, JG 2's two *Gruppen* were instructed to find a more suitable advanced landing ground in occupied French territory. Leutnant Temme again;

'The *Kommandeur* and I flew ahead to inspect an airfield near Charleville. It was full of bomb holes. We landed carefully between the craters. Unfortunately, the field quickly filled up with machines of another *Geschwader* (JG 27), and we were forced to look elsewhere. There was another French landing ground nearby at Signy le Petit. But it was surrounded by dense woods, and these were reportedly still full of enemy troops.

'I therefore returned to Bastogne and quickly organised a *Kommando* of ten men. We were flown into Signy by a Ju 52 transport, which promptly departed the moment we had climbed out of it. There we were, all alone with a few automatic weapons and some provisions. Our orders: to prepare the field for the arrival of the *Geschwader*, and to clear the nearby woods of any French stragglers.'

A trawl through the trees bordering the landing strip netted Temme and his ten-men *Kommando* more than they had bargained for – a corps commander, three divisional generals and some 200 French colonial troops! Deciding that discretion was the better part of valour, the 11 of them set about dismantling a pair of machine guns from the wreckage of

Once the woods in the background had been cleared of French stragglers, the atmosphere at Signy le Petit became rather more relaxed. The pilot on the right is Feldwebel Willinger, who, six months hence, would score the *Geschwader's* 500th victory

The campaign in France was not a complete picnic. Although only three aircraft were lost, many more were damaged to varying degrees, including 1. *Staffel's* 'White 5'. Photographed in one of those ubiquitous French cornfields sometime in May, the aircraft seems to have suffered quite severe damage. By this time JG 2's early *Emils* were undergoing another change of camouflage, the pale hellblau surfaces now being darkened with a variety of hand-applied dense dapple finishes. For some reason, the five victory bars on the fighter's tailfin appear to have been crudely overpainted – perhaps a recent change of ownership?

one of the many French aircraft littering the field and proceeded to barricade themselves in for the night in the top storey of a neighbouring farmhouse while business went on as usual below – the building doubled as the local bar and brothel!

As the tempo of the ground advance quickened, so the list of JG 2's victories lengthened. On 17 May I. *Gruppe* claimed the destruction of seven French bombers, four being described as LeO 45s and the remainder as LeO 451s. The latter trio were all credited to 3. *Staffel's* Leutnant Helmut Wick. Twenty-four hours later it was the RAF which was providing the opposition, and sustaining the casualties – seven Blenheims and a single Lysander fell to the guns of the *'Richthofen'* pilots.

19 May's 12 claims were all fighters, divided equally between RAF Hurricanes and *Armée de l'Air* Moranes. But this day also saw the loss of Leutnant Werner Grübel of 1. *Staffel*, who failed to return from a sortie in the Cambrai area.

Two kills by Oberfeldwebel Werner Machold on the evening of 20 May – a Blenheim and a Hurricane, both over Péronne – took the *Geschwader's*

Preparing for a mission, *Geschwaderkommodore* von Bülow-Bothkamp gets a helping hand with his kapok life-jacket and flare pistol. His machine has also been subject to liberal – and none too careful – dappling

Hauptmann Alexander von Winterfeldt of 3./JG 2 is welcomed back at Beaulieu by members of the groundcrew after a successful May sortie. His three kills (a Blenheim, a Morane MS.406 and a LeO 45) that month were achieved on consecutive days, beginning on 18 May

total score since the beginning of the *Blitzkrieg* in the west to 100. An announcement to this effect was made in an official communiqué (although post-war research puts the truer figure – discounting the attached I./JG 76's successes – as nearer the 80 mark).

Werner Machold also contributed two Moranes to the nine victories claimed in the Compiegne region on 21 May. Another of the French fighters fell to Major Dr Erich Mix, *Gruppenkommandeur* of III./JG 2. But in the melée, Mix's own machine was hit and set on fire. Despite being wounded, he managed to bail out. Hiding by day and walking by night, the 42-year-old World War 1 veteran reached the German lines on 23 May, and was soon back with his *Gruppe*.

By this time the spearheads of 2. *Panzerdivision* had reached the Channel coast north of Abbeville. The withdrawal of the RAF Component from France was underway, and the even more ambitious evacuation of the encircled BEF from Dunkirk was about to begin.

It was on 26 May that JG 2 'Richthofen' first clashed with UK-based RAF Spitfires – aircraft whose graceful shape and elliptical planform would become all too familiar in the years ahead. That indefatigable diarist Paul Temme takes up the story;

'Stuka attack against the citadel at Calais and shipping offshore. I am to fly cover with 2. *Staffel*. It's 220 km (136 miles) from Signy to the Channel coast! There won't be much time left for dogfighting when we get there. Over Calais we bump into a Blenheim, which is immediately despatched by Leutnant Hoffmann.

'Just as the Stukas begin to dive on the ships, English Spitfires appear in great numbers. We are eight against 20. A vicious free-for-all develops. Time and again the Spitfires try to get at the Stukas, but Oberleutnant Bethke, leader of the attack *Schwarm*, keeps them well at bay.

The 'black men' (groundcrew) and the recovery teams were the unsung heroes who kept the *Geschwader* flying. 9./JG 2's 'Yellow 6' is brought back to base in something of a sorry state . . .

. . . but work is soon underway to put things right, including a complete engine change . . .

. . . and 'Yellow 6' is back in the air again – but is it the same *Emil*. A close examination of the original prints reveals that the swastika has moved from the rudder hinge-line to the tailfin

'I also get in a few bursts, the only result being that the Spitfire I am aiming at quickly sheers away and disappears from sight. Then I am attacked by two more Spitfires. One gets on my tail. But he's a lousy shot. I let him sit there while I call up my wingman, Feldwebel Leipelt, on the R/T. He bores in to close range and sends the Spitfire down in flames. Bravo Leipelt!

'The dogfight against the Tommies lasts a little while longer and then our fuel situation forces us to break off the action. We and the Stukas all reach home safely. Five kills! Including one to me!'

I./JG 2's likely opponents, No 19 Sqn, did indeed lose four Spitfires in the Calais area on this date, with a fifth force-landing on the Kent coast.

Later that same afternoon Temme was back over Calais, this time flying with 1. *Staffel*. He shot down a second Spitfire during this mission. By day's end I./JG 2 had claimed ten Spitfires in all (plus Heinz Hoffmann's Blenheim). III./JG 2 came a poor second on this date with two Moranes downed over Amiens.

There followed a 48-hour lull. JG 2's next two victories were not achieved until the evening of 29 May, both pilots claiming – somewhat mystifyingly – that their victims had been Westland Wapitis!

With the epic Dunkirk evacuation nearing completion, the first phase of the assault in the west – code-named 'Case Yellow' – was all but over. Holland and Belgium had capitulated. Most of the British had been driven from mainland Europe, and now the second stage of the grand plan – 'Case Red', the thrust south-westward into the heart of France – could begin.

On 1 June 1940 I. and III./JG 2 moved forward from Signy-le-Petit to Couvron, near Laon. Throughout the first half of June the *'Richthofen' Gruppen* would continue to operate as before, flying a mixture of *freie Jagd* and escort duties. But during this closing chapter of the *Blitzkrieg* in the west, their opponents – and their victories – would be almost exclusively French. Some 60 *Armée de l'Air* machines would fall to their guns. Several names already mentioned, the likes of Hahn, Machold and Rudorffer,

Gefreiter Hans Tilley of 3./JG 2 was one of the two pilots claiming 'Westland Wapitis' on 29 May (the other was 'Ku–Vo' Votel). As these were first victories for both of them, excitement perhaps played its part. On reflection, their victims were probably Lysanders (which featured regularly on the *Geschwader's* scoreboard during this period). Incidentally, this photograph of Tilley was taken immediately prior to the *Blitzkrieg*, possibly at Bassenheim – that distinctive 'notch' in the tree-line to the right of the aerial mast looks rather familiar (see the top photograph on page 32)

Members of 7. ***Staffel*** **inspect a common adversary of their advance through France – a Curtiss Hawk H-75 of the *Armée de l'Air***

Aircraft of 3./JG 2 on the prowl high above the French countryside. The pilots are (from left to right), Lt Franz Fiby, Fw Fritz Stritzel, Olt Jobst Hauenschild (lead), Ofw Erwin Kley and Ofw Franz Jänisch

would consolidate their growing status with multiple victories on single missions. But for one man above all others – Helmut Wick – the coming fortnight's drive through France would provide the springboard for his rise to national fame.

'Case Red' was launched on 3 June with Operation *Paula* – a massed bombing raid on airfields and armament factories in the Greater Paris area. JG 2 downed seven French fighters on this date. But the Luftwaffe did not escape entirely without loss either. The *Geschwader's* previous *Kommodore*, Oberst von Massow (now serving as *Jafü 3*) had gone along to witness the results of the attack – or perhaps to cast a critical eye on his pilots' performance?

Some 12 miles (20 km) north of Paris, von Massow's Bf 109 was hit by French anti-aircraft fire and he was forced to take to his parachute. But, like Dr Mix before him, he managed to evade capture and make his way back to the German lines – those veterans were certainly made of stern stuff!

On 4 June Hauptmann Schellmann's II. *Gruppe* was released from its detachment to *Luftflotte 2* in Belgium and flew in to Monceau-le-Vast, also near Laon. At long last, after more than nine months of hostilities, the *Jagdgeschwader 'Richthofen'* was finally able to field its three component *Gruppen* as a single entity.

The attached I./JG 76, which had amassed 60 victories of its own while under von Bülow's control, departed the following day, subsequently to be redesignated II./JG 54.

5 and 6 June were by far the most successful days for the *Geschwader* in the second half of the campaign against France. During these 48 hours, in a sprawling series of engagements to the north-east of the enemy's capital, the three *Gruppen* between them accounted for no fewer than 41 French aircraft against a single loss – that of 2. *Staffel's* Leutnant Eberhardt von Reden.

This not only raised JG 2's combined total to 200 (an overclaim by some ten per cent), it also boosted Helmut Wick's score into double figures.

3. *Staffel* had flown three missions on 5 June. It was during the last of these, while escorting ground-attack aircraft to targets near Noyon, that they encountered a formation of 30+ Bloch 151s. Wick shot down four of the radial-engined French fighters in a dogfight lasting just 12 minutes. He had doubled his score to eight (plus two unconfirmed) in a single engagement.

Wick flew another three missions the following day. And again it was during the final sortie that he was successful, as described by his wingman Leutnant Franz Fiby;

'On 6 June our *Schwarm* was attached to 2. *Staffel* to provide cover for a reconnaissance sortie (Do 17) in the Rheims area. After about 20 minutes' flying time, Moranes were reported approaching. After that it didn't stop: "Ahead to the left, same altitude, 6 Moranes". "High right, 8 Blochs", and so on, and so on.

'We climbed from 3000 metres (9850 ft) up to 7500 (24,500) where the air was a bit clearer. Below us were about 40 French fighters. My *Schwarmführer* positioned us up sun and waited for the right moment.

Leutnant Franz Fiby claimed his first kill (a Bloch fighter) on 6 June while flying wingman to Helmut Wick. Like the earlier photograph of Hans Tilley, this shot was also taken before the *Blitzkrieg* began – during January, in fact – and on the same machine. Serving as 3. *Staffel's* reserve aircraft, 'Yellow 13' was obviously a favourite perch on which to have one's picture taken. A parachute on the wing added an extra touch of authenticity!

'The enemy were flying in a loose defensive circle. Helmut (Wick) selected a target, winged over into a dive and "had a quick sniff at his trousers" (got on his tail). But the Frenchman pulled a violent left turn and skidded away. I was right behind Helmut and was equally unsuccessful.

'Using our excess of speed, and thanks to our willing engines, we zoomed back upwards and soon regained the 700 metres (2300 ft) we had squandered.

'Meanwhile, down below, they continued doggedly circling. What they hoped to achieve was anybody's guess. They would have done better to clear off.

'Our *Schwarm* quickly reassembled. Fränzchen (Oberfeldwebel Franz Jänisch) and "Ku-Vo" (Leutnant Kurt Votel) would remain upstairs as cover while Helmut and I dived back down for another try.

'As I closed in on my Bloch, I could see Helmut sitting on the tail of his chosen victim, his guns hammering. The Frenchman turned on his back. At first I thought he was shamming and was about to roll away. But no, the roll quickly developed into an uncontrollable dive which only ended when the machine smashed into the ground far below.

'I was still sitting behind my Bloch (152), which was in a gentle left-hand turn. I remained on his tail long enough to see him start to go down. But it takes an awfully long time for such a crate to fall to earth from 6000 metres (20,000 ft).

'By now the other two were attacking the Blochs. But "Ku-Vo's" radiator was leaking badly. I called him up: "Achtung! You're leaving a white trail – radiator hit". But he obviously didn't hear me in the heat of the chase. Later he was just able to make it back to base, gliding in with a dead engine.

'Great excitement back at *Staffel* dispersal when our four machines of 3. *Schwarm* landed and reported five kills without loss. Helmut, of course, had to go one better than the rest of us by getting a double.'

After 6 June targets became harder to find. Helmut Wick claimed another double – a Bloch and a Morane – again over Rheims on the evening of 8 June. He was also responsible for JG 2's last two confirmed RAF kills of the French campaign, downing a Blenheim (possibly of No 107 Sqn) near Soissons on 9 June, and a Battle in the Provins region four days later. That same 13 June also saw another future *'Richthofen' Kommodore* first make his mark when 6. *Staffel's* Leutnant Egon Mayer claimed the destruction of a Morane fighter.

13 June was the date, too, when all three *Gruppen* first shared a common field by flying in to Oulchy-le-Chateau, approximately midway between Rheims and Paris. During the 72 hours they spent there, Oberleutnant Heinz Greisert of 2./JG 2 shot down a Hawk H-75. This kill, early on the morning of 15 June, was to be the last of the 185 victories credited to the *Geschwader* since the launch of the *Blitzkrieg* in the west five weeks earlier.

On 16 June the entire *Geschwader* transferred some 50 miles (80 km) south to Marigny-le-Chatel.

Hauptmann Roth, the *Gruppenkommandeur* of I./JG 2, who had been in poor health for some time, was transferred to the RLM on 22 June. His place was taken by Hauptmann Hennig Strümpell, a *Legion Condor* veteran and erstwhile *Kapitän* of 3. *Staffel*. This, in turn, left vacant the leadership of 3./JG 2. And there was one within its ranks who was ideally suited to fill the post. *Kommodore* von Bülow-Bothkamp certainly had no hesitation;

'It gives me great pleasure, Herr Oberleutnant Wick, to appoint you herewith to the position of *Staffelführer*. Official confirmation to the office of *Staffelkapitän* will no doubt follow very shortly. I wanted to be the first to wish you *"Hals-und Beinbruch"* in this new undertaking.'

At 0035 hours on 25 June the cease-fire was sounded. The Battle of France had been won. Two days later JG 2 was transferred to Evreux, west of Paris. Its men were not to enjoy the amenities of this established base for very long, for it was scheduled for occupation by the Ju 88 bombers of I./KG 54. Ordered to vacate Evreux, *Jagdgeschwader 'Richthofen'* was assigned alternative accommodation some 16 miles (25 km) to the west – a large cornfield!

Following an early morning patrol, *Staffelkapitän* Helmut Wick's *Schwarm* from 3./JG 2 was given the job of reconnoitring the new site. The man who faced the unenviable task of attempting the first landing was Oberfeldwebel Franz Jänisch;

'As we approached the area indicated on our maps it was seen to be just a huge field of grain. There was nothing to suggest even a landing strip, let alone a proper airfield. And not a sign of any activity either.

'I called Helmut to let him know that I was going to try to land in the corn (which turned out to be over one metre (3 ft) high) and that he should keep an eye out for any possible hazards. As Wick circled overhead I put her down gently but safely. At this point a German truck appeared.'

The remainder of the *Schwarm* landed one after the other in Jänisch's tracks, guided in by the narrow swathe his propeller had scythed through the standing crop. There was no possibility of their taking off again. But the ground party, which had arrived in the truck, managed to flatten – not cut – a large expanse of corn to allow the rest of I. *Gruppe* to fly in the following day.

Such were the humble beginnings of Beaumont-le-Roger airfield (named after the nearby township), which was to become the *Jagdgeschwader 'Richthofen's'* main base, and spiritual home, for the next four years. An elegant – if somewhat rat-infested – chateau in the trees bordering the field, plus another down in the town, provided for the creature comforts. In the course of time a hutted encampment and workshops

The chateau in the town of Beaumont-le-Roger, which was the home of the Duchesse de Magenta, served as *Geschwader* HQ until it was totally destroyed by B-17s on 28 June 1943

Franz Jänisch's 'Yellow 8' (Wk-Nr 1588) – the aircraft in which he first touched down at Beaumont. His personal 'Mickey Mouse' emblem (a momento of his time with 3.J/88 in Spain as Werner Mölders' wingman) can just be made out ahead of the fuselage numeral. 'Yellow 8' ended its operational career in a far less successful landing, for after being shot up by RAF fighters, it was put down on its belly on the Isle of Wight by Feldwebel Horst Hellriegel on 15 October 1940 – much to its 'proper' owner's intense annoyance!

sprang up under the cover of the trees, a row of earth and timber blast walls was constructed along the perimeter track to serve as dispersal pens for the aircraft, and a large wooden command centre and operational HQ building were erected.

But all this lay in the future. For the moment there were more urgent priorities to hand. Having rejected the peace feelers extended by the Führer at the conclusion of the *Blitzkrieg* in the west, British Prime Minister Winston Churchill summed up the immediate situation in just over a dozen words;

'The Battle of France is over. The Battle of Britain is about to begin.'

THE BATTLE OF BRITAIN

Despite the British Premier's defiant words, and forecast of imminent onslaught, there was a short but distinct lull after the end of the fighting in France and before the first serious air attacks were launched against southern England.

As *Reichsmarschall* Göring began, almost leisurely, to assemble his forces along the Channel coast, many frontline units – including elements of JG 2 – enjoyed the luxury of brief rotation back to Germany to make good the losses and depredations suffered in the recent campaigning.

If Hauptmann Strümpell's I. *Gruppe* did, as some sources suggest, return to Berlin, their stay must have been brief in the extreme, for by the first week of July they were operational out of Beaumont-le-Roger. One of their first cross-Channel forays was a Stuka-escort mission against the Portland naval base on the evening of 9 July.

During the course of this mission the unit lost one of their charges to a No 609 Sqn Spitfire up from nearby Warmwell, but redressed the balance by shooting down another of that squadron's fighters during the encounter (Spitfire I R6657, flown by Flg Off P Drummond-Hay, who was killed). In fact, two pilots – future *Experte* Leutnant Anton Mader of the *Gruppenstab* and 1. *Staffel's* Unteroffizier Willi Reins – were each credited with a Spitfire south of Portland at exactly the same time: 2030 hours. Just who the successful claimant was on this occasion was impossible to determine. But No 609's Spitfires would become regular adversaries of JG 2 in the weeks and months which lay ahead.

A little over a week later, on 17 July, Helmut Wick scored his first Battle of Britain victory – a Spitfire off Brighton. This was almost certainly No 64 Sqn's P9507, which a wounded Flg Off Don 'Butch' Taylor crash-landed at Hailsham. He had been on a convoy patrol at the time, and subsequently reported that he had failed to see his assailant at any stage during the brief engagement.

The following day, while Oberleutnant Heinz Greisert of I. *Gruppenstab* was claiming a Spitfire off the Isle of Wight, II./JG 2 entered the fray on the French side of the Channel. *Gruppenkommandeur* Wolfgang Schellmann and Unteroffizier Willi Melchert each downed a Blenheim (both from No 236 Sqn), which were undertaking photographic reconnaissance missions off Le Havre.

JG 2's next four victories were also Blenheims, which were all claimed in the same area. Feldwebel Siegfried Schnell of 4. *Staffel* reportedly got one on each of two consecutive days, 29 and 30 July. On 2 August Oberleutnant Paul Temme, now *Gruppen-Adjutant* of I./JG 2, was the next to score;

'The *Stabskette* was the last to take off. I was flying the third machine. While circling Le Havre I saw a Blenheim suddenly appear out of the 200-metre (650-ft) cloud base. It immediately tried to dodge back into cover. I gave chase, wondering for an instant whether it was perhaps a Ju 88.

'It vanished into a cloud but I kept after it. The rear gunner opened up and I returned his fire. Again it disappeared. I remained on its tail, shooting all the while. Damn! Cannon stoppage! But at that moment the Engländer's right engine burst into flames.

'Once more it sought cloud cover. This time I let it go, thinking it wouldn't get very far. Then I saw it spinning down on fire. I was quite close as it crashed into the main street of Le Havre, exploded and blazed fiercely. I could see the burning fuel running along the gutters and the tram lines. A few minutes later the bombs detonated, causing severe damage to the surrounding buildings.'

Temme later drove to the scene of the crash. All that remained were the two engines. And, as he had feared, there were civilian casualties – three people had been killed by the exploding bombs.

The identity of Temme's victim remains something of a mystery – unless it was the No 139 Sqn aircraft sent to bomb Luftwaffe airfields, and which was presumed lost over the Channel on 3 August. But there is little doubt concerning the Blenheim claimed by 1. *Staffel's* Feldwebel Rudolf Täschner north of Le Havre late in the afternoon of 4 August. This was another No 236 Sqn machine – more fortunate than its fellows of some three weeks earlier – which, although severely damaged by Täschner's attack, managed to make it back to England.

On that same 4 August Major Dr Mix's III. *Gruppe* is reported to have returned to France after more than a month spent in Frankfurt. Big as Beaumont's cornfield was, its facilities were still extremely rudimentary. For this reason – or perhaps to counter the recent upsurge of RAF interest in the area – III./JG 2 was ordered to take up residence at Octeville, on the outskirts of Le Havre, which had previously been used only by the forward *Alarmstaffeln*.

This early *Emil* (an E-1 with an E-4 canopy) of 7./JG 2 displays both its sponge(?)-applied dapple camouflage and its *Staffel* badge. The latter dates back to the pre-*Blitzkrieg* period when Prime Minister Neville Chamberlain, and not Winston Churchill, was the arch-enemy. It is based on 7./JG 2's motto – a piece of doggerel which translates roughly as, 'The thumb of the Seventh presses in the old hat of Chamberlain'

Exactly one week later, on 11 August, all three *Gruppen* participated in the largest raid yet sent against Britain. Again the target was to be the naval base at Portland. Staging via Cherbourg, JG 2 began taking-off at 1055 hours to lead the bombers of KGs 27 and 54 to their objective some 70 miles (112 km) away across the Channel. This was the first time the *Geschwader* had been fully committed. In just over one hour its pilots would have scored JG 2's greatest success, and suffered their heaviest losses, of any single day in the Battle.

Flying in the van of the leading formations, the *Geschwader's* orders were to 'suppress the British fighters for 35 minutes whatever the cost'. It was easier said than done. Tracking the incoming raid on radar, the RAF vectored aircraft of at least eight squadrons to the scene. The enormous dogfight which ensued extended across the width of Weymouth Bay.

As other Bf 109s arrived to cover the raiders' withdrawal, JG 2 broke off the engagement shortly after midday and headed back to France. Seven aircraft failed to return, whilst an eighth crashed near Cherbourg. Five pilots, including one *Gruppen-Adjutant* and one *Staffelkapitän*, were reported killed or missing.

For their part, the pilots of the *Geschwader* had claimed no fewer than 22 kills. Many familiar names added one or more victories to their scores on this day, Erich Rudorffer being credited with two and Helmut Wick three. But there were newcomers too, such as 8. *Staffel's* Oberleutnant Bruno Stolle and Feldwebel Kurt Goltzsch. The former downed a brace of Spitfires over Portland in just four minutes, whilst the latter despatched a Hurricane on the outermost fringe of the dogfight near Swanage.

Given the ferocity of the clash, aircraft recognition was understandably not of the highest order. For example, Werner Machold jumped the gun somewhat by identifying his victim as a Tomahawk – a type which would not enter RAF squadron service in the UK for another 12 months. And perhaps it was just force of habit which convinced Helmut Wick that one of his trio of kills was a Hawk H-75!

Compared to the 11 August action, *'Adlertag'*, launched 48 hours later, was something of an anti-climax for JG 2. 'Eagle Day' was intended to be the final knockout blow which would sweep the RAF from the skies of southern England, and thus pave the way for invasion. But it didn't quite work out that way. A combination of bad weather in the early hours of 13

On 13 August Oberleutnant Paul Temme was brought down in a cornfield alongside Shoreham airfield (which lies just behind the railway embankment in the background) after an engagement with Hurricanes. Although missing its canopy, and with its propeller blades badly bent out of shape, Temme's Bf 109E-4 appears to otherwise intact

August and a series of last-minute recalls to units either on the point of taking off or already aloft – some of which were heeded, some not – completely fragmented the Luftwaffe's plans.

Among the aircraft which did set off across the Channel early on the morning of *'Adlertag'* were a dozen fighters of I./JG 2. After take-off from Beaumont at 0700 hours, they split into three *Schwärme* to carry out *freie Jagd* sweeps along the English south coast. Paul Temme and Werner Machold each claimed a Hurricane near Brighton, but then Temme's own machine was hit – probably by a No 43 Sqn Hurricane – and he was forced to belly land in a cornfield (a real home away from home!) close alongside Shoreham aerodrome.

During the course of the next fortnight further *freie Jagd* and bomber escort missions cost JG 2 another two PoWs (both *Staffelkapitäne* from II. *Gruppe*), twice that number killed or missing, plus many more wounded.

But unit and individual scores were mounting too. The nine kills claimed over the Weymouth area on the evening of 25 August pushed the *Geschwader's* total passed the 250-figure, and included Helmut Wick's 20th confirmed victory. With 20 enemy aircraft destroyed then being the benchmark for the award of the Knight's Cross, Oberleutnant Wick was duly presented with this prestigious decoration on 27 August. He was, in fact, the second member of JG 2 to receive the Knight's Cross, for *Kommodore* von Bülow-Bothkamp had been similarly honoured – for outstanding leadership – just five days earlier.

The raid by some 50 He 111s against Portsmouth on 26 August – during which JG 2's escorting fighters were credited with five kills – would prove to be the last major daylight attack by (*text continues on page 62*)

Towards the end of August JG 2's Bf 109s began to sport their now famous 'yellow noses'. This III. *Gruppe* machine, seen basking in the sun in a wooded corner at Le Havre/Octeville, has a newly-painted cowling and spinner. Indeed, they are so pristine one can almost smell the fresh paint

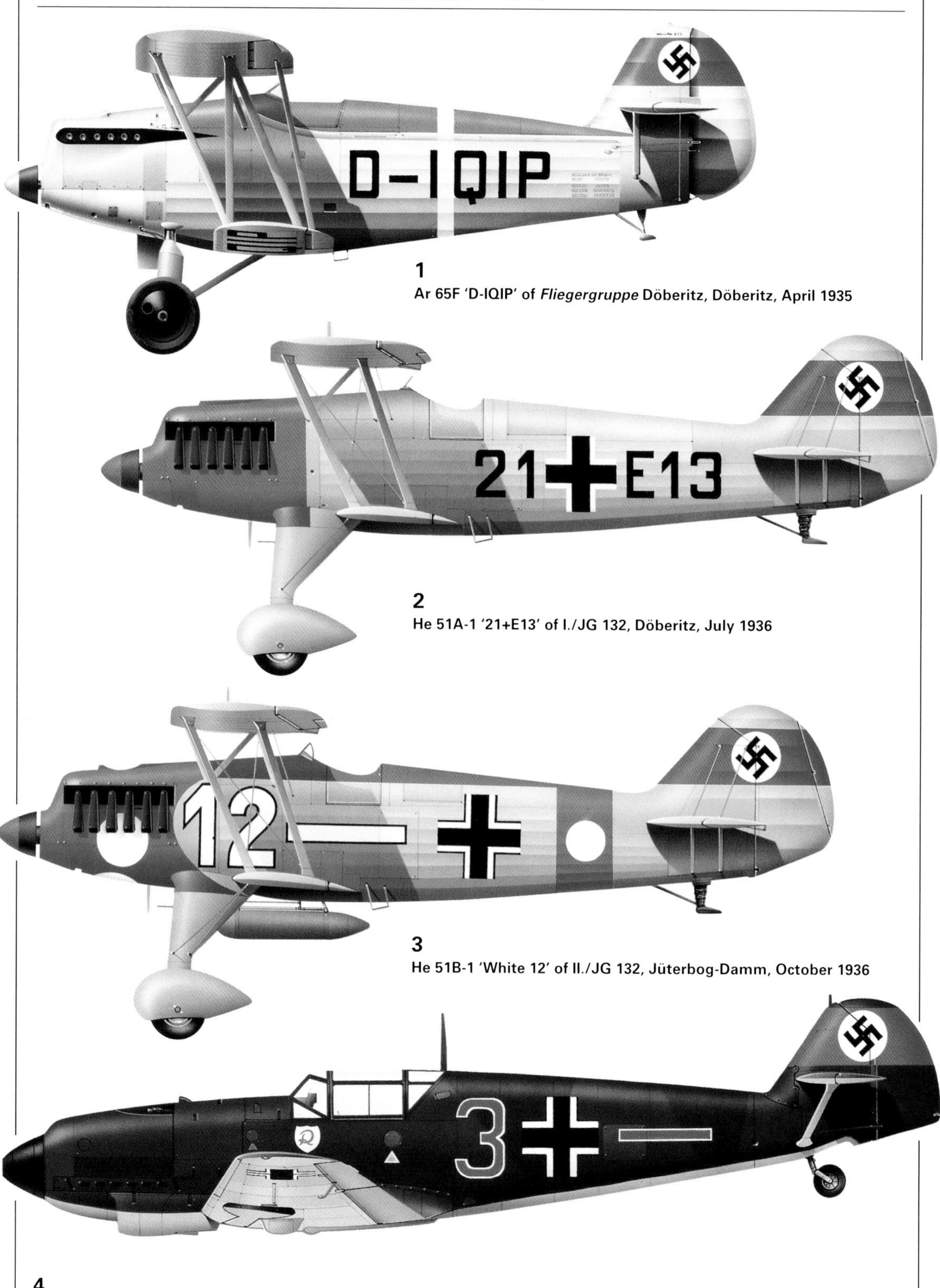

1
Ar 65F 'D-IQIP' of *Fliegergruppe* Döberitz, Döberitz, April 1935

2
He 51A-1 '21+E13' of I./JG 132, Döberitz, July 1936

3
He 51B-1 'White 12' of II./JG 132, Jüterbog-Damm, October 1936

4
Bf 109B-2 'Red 3' of II./JG 132, Jüterbog-Damm, August 1937

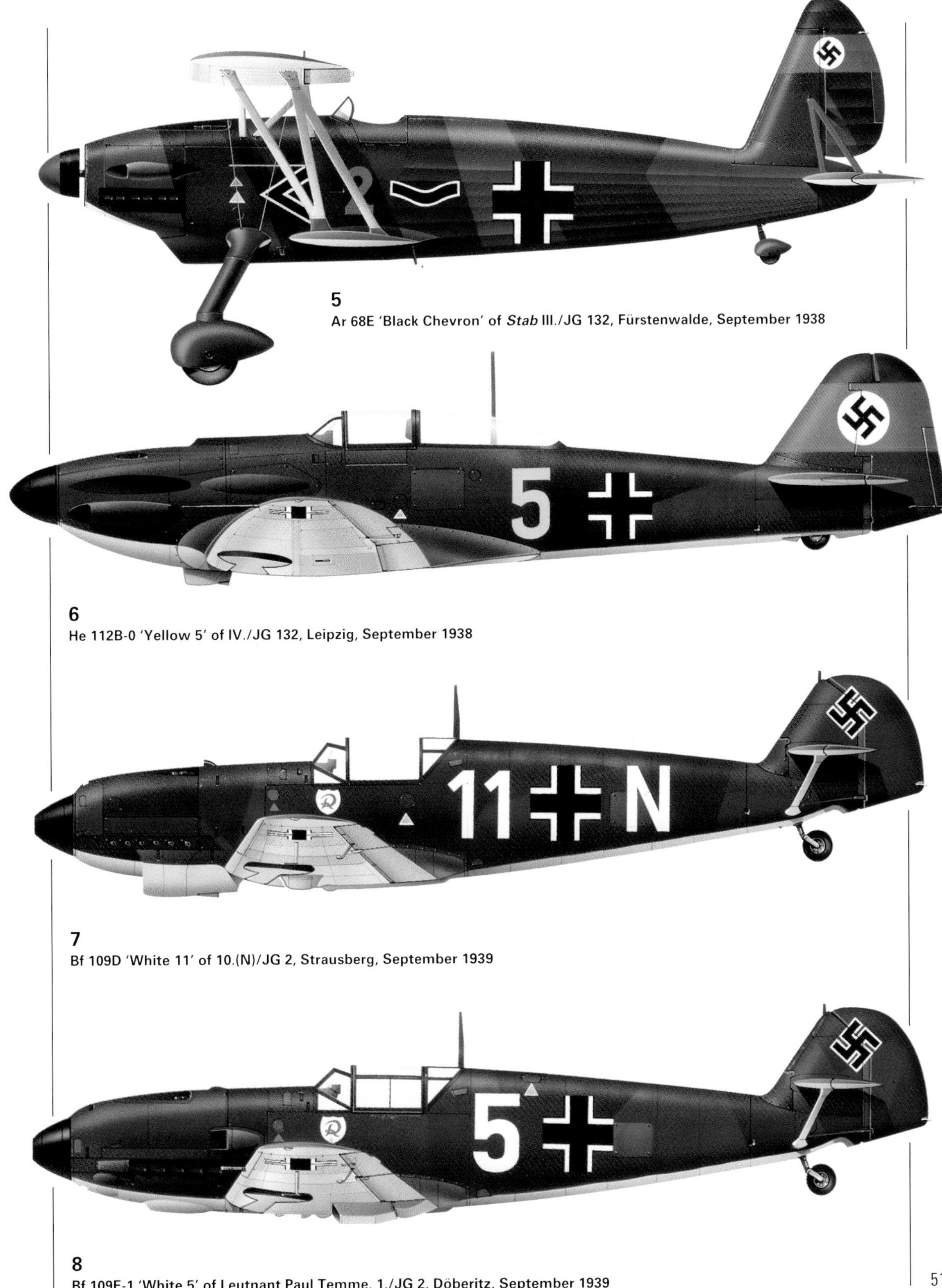

5
Ar 68E 'Black Chevron' of *Stab* III./JG 132, Fürstenwalde, September 1938

6
He 112B-0 'Yellow 5' of IV./JG 132, Leipzig, September 1938

7
Bf 109D 'White 11' of 10.(N)/JG 2, Strausberg, September 1939

8
Bf 109E-1 'White 5' of Leutnant Paul Temme, 1./JG 2, Döberitz, September 1939

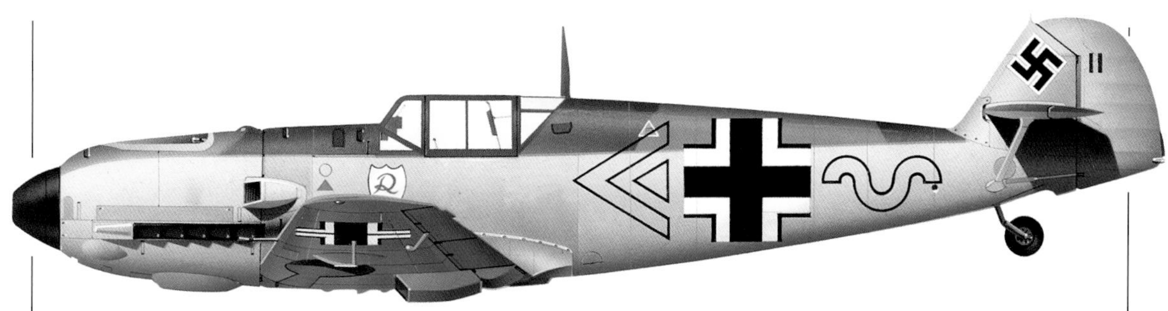

9
Bf 109E-3 'Chevron-Triangle' of Major Dr Erich Mix, *Gruppenkommandeur* III./JG 2, France, May 1940

10
Bf 109E-3 'Yellow 8' of Unteroffizier Rudolf Rothenfelder, 9./JG 2, Le Havre/Octeville, August 1940

11
Bf 109E-3 'White 8' of Oberfeldwebel Kurt Goltzsch, 7./JG 2, Cherbourg-Théville, September 1940

12
Bf 109E-4 'Red 1' of 8./JG 2, Oye-Plage, September 1940

13
Bf 109E-4 'Black Double Chevron' of Hauptmann Helmut Wick, *Gruppenkommandeur* of I./JG 2, Beaumont-le-Roger, October 1940

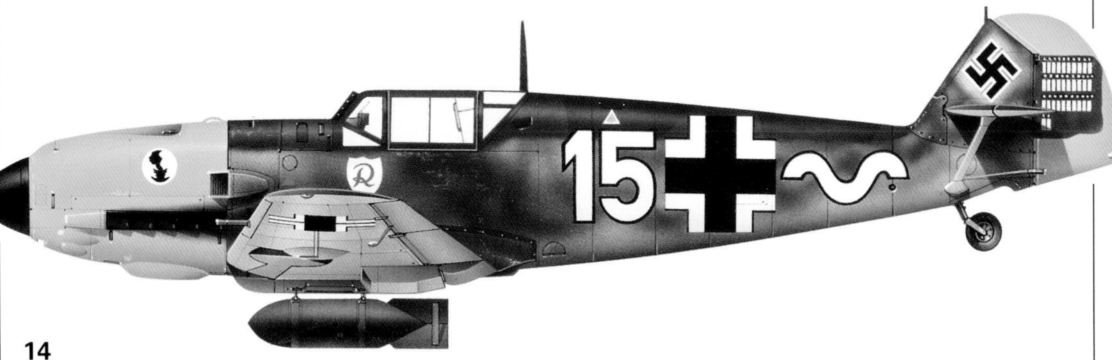

14
Bf 109E-7 'White 15' of Oberleutnant Werner Machold, *Staffelkapitän* 7./JG 2, Caen-Rocquancourt, May 1941

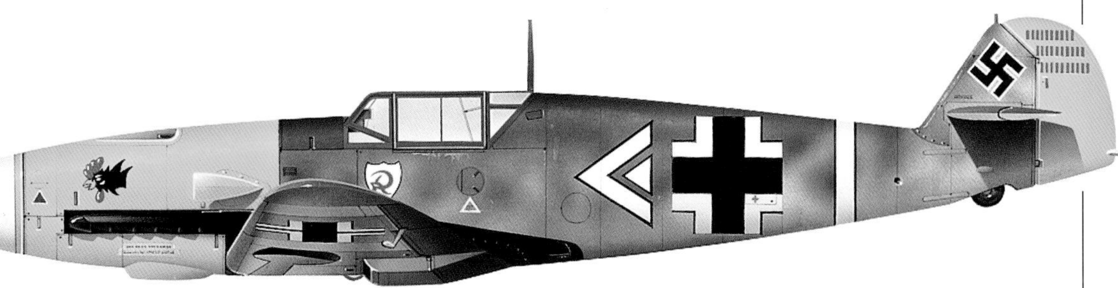

15
Bf 109F-2 'White Double Chevron' of Hauptmann Hans Hahn, *Gruppenkommandeur* III./JG 2, St Pol, Summer 1941

16
Bf 109F-2 'White 1' of Oberleutnant Egon Mayer, *Staffelkapitän* 7./JG 2, St Pol, Summer 1941

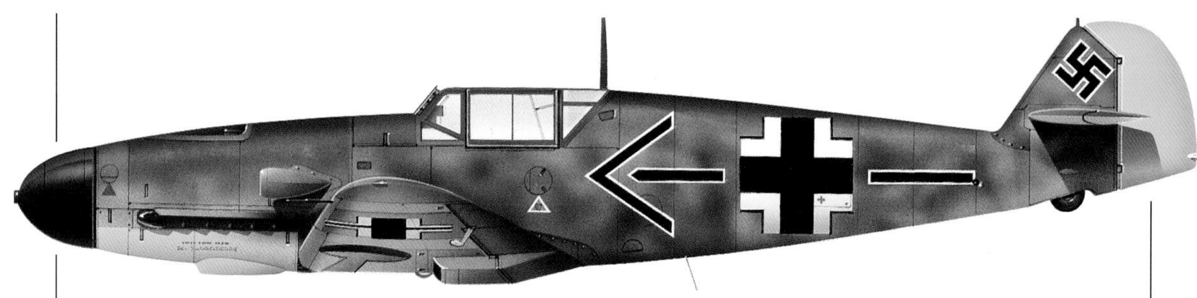

17
Bf 109F-4 'Black Chevron and Bars' of Major Walter Oesau, *Geschwaderkommodore* JG 2, St.Pol, Autumn 1941

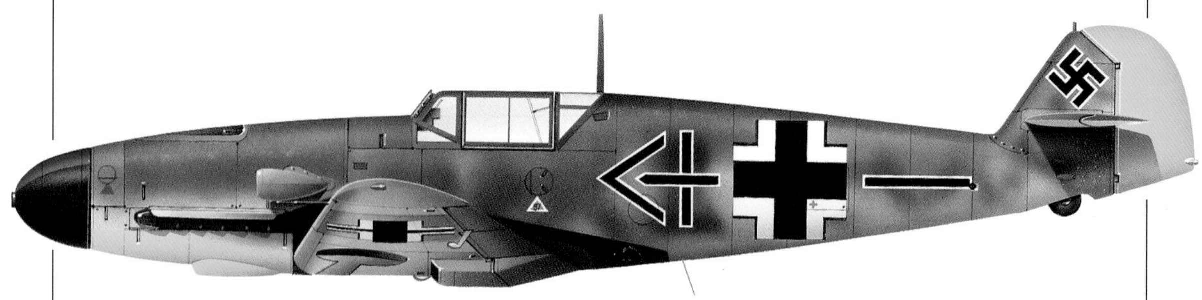

18
Bf 109F-4 'Black Chevron and Crossed Bar(s)' of Oberleutnant Erich Leie, *Geschwader-Adjutant* JG 2, St Pol, Autumn 1941

19
Bf 109F-4 'Black Bars and Dot' of Oberleutnant Rudolf Pflanz, *Geschwader-TO* JG 2, St Pol, Autumn 1941

20
Bf 109F-4 'Yellow 9' of Oberleutnant Erich Rudorffer, *Staffelkapitän* 6./JG 2, Abbeville-Drucat, Autumn 1941

21

Bf 109F-4/B 'Blue 1 Chevron and Bar' of Oberleutnant Frank Liesendahl, *Staffelkapitän* 10. (*Jabo*)/ JG 2, Beaumont-le-Roger, April 1942

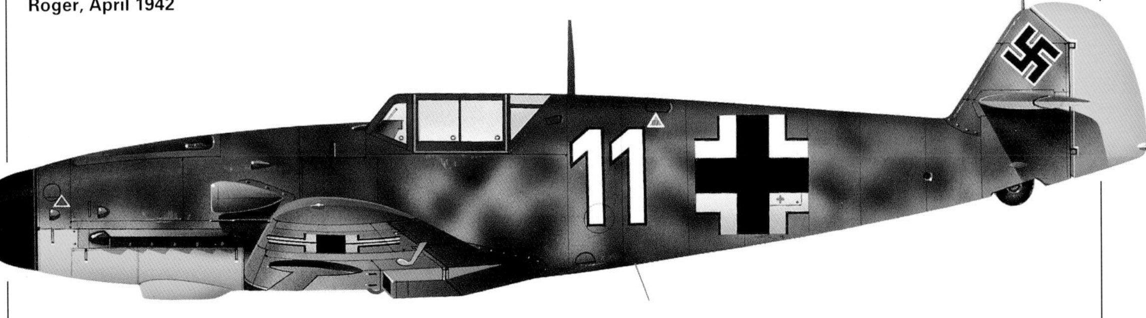

22

Bf 109G-1 'White 11' of Oberleutnant Julius Meimberg, *Staffelkapitän* 11./JG 2, Poix, Summer 1942

23

Fw 190A-2 'Yellow 13' of Oberfeldwebel Josef Heinzeller, 3./JG 2, Triqueville, June 1942

24

Fw 190A-3 'Black Bars and Crossbar' of Leutnant Hubert von Greim, *Stab* JG 2, Triqueville, Summer 1942

25

Fw 190A-3 'Yellow 1' of Oberleutnant Erich Rudorffer, *Staffelkapitän* 6./JG 2, Beaumont-le-Roger, August 1942

26

Fw 190A-3 'White Double Chevron' of Hauptmann Hans Hahn, *Gruppenkommandeur* III./JG 2, Poix, September 1942

27

Fw 190A-4 'White 1' of Oberleutnant Kurt Bühligen, *Staffelkapitän* 4./JG 2, Kairouan/Tunisia, December 1942

28

Fw 190A-4 'Black Double Chevron' of Oberleutnant Adolf Dickfeld, *Gruppenkommandeur* II./JG 2, Kairouan/Tunisia, January 1943

29
Fw 190A-4 'Yellow 4' of Hauptmann Siegfried Schnell, *Staffelkapitän* of 9./JG 2, Vannes, February 1943

30
Fw 190A-4 'Black Rectangle and Bars' of Oberstleutnant Walter Oesau, *Geschwaderkommodore* JG 2, Beaumont-le-Roger, February 1943

31
Fw 190A-4 'Black 1' of Oberleutnant Horst Hannig, *Staffelkapitän* 2./JG 2, Triqueville, Spring 1943

32
Fw 190A-5 'White Double Chevron' of Hauptmann Egon Mayer, *Gruppenkommandeur* III./JG 2, Cherbourg-Théville, Spring 1943

33

Fw 190A-4 'Green 13' of Oberstleutnant Walter Oesau, *Geschwaderkommodore* JG 2, Beaumont-le-Roger, June 1943

34

Fw 190A-6 'Yellow 2' of Oberleutnant Josef Wurmheller, *Staffelkapitän* 9./JG 2, Vannes, September 1943

35

Bf 109G-6 'White 2' of 4./JG 2, Evreux, Autumn 1943

36

Bf 109G-6 'Blue 6' of 8./JG 2, Creil, April 1944

37
Fw 190A-8 'Black Double Chevron and Bars' of Major Bühligen, *Geschwaderkommodore* JG 2, Creil June 1944

38
Bf 109G-14 'Black 8' of 5./JG 2, Ettingshausen, December 1944

39
Fw 190D-9 'Yellow 11' of II./JG 2, Stockheim, March 1945

40
Fw 190D-9 'White 4' of JG 2, Straubing, May 1945

1
JG 2 *'Richthofen'*
worn below the windscreen on Bf 109B, C, D, E and F

2
III./JG 2
worn on the cowling of Bf 109F and Fw 190A

3
1./JG 2
worn on the cowling of Bf 109G

4
3./JG 2
worn on the cowling of Bf 109E

5
7./JG 2
worn on the cowling of Bf 109E/F and Fw 190A

6
8./JG 2
worn on the cowling of Bf 109E

7
9./JG 2
worn on the cowling of Bf 109E/F

8
10.(*Jabo*)/JG 2
worn on the cowling of Bf 109F and Fw 190A

9
10.(N)/JG 2
worn on the cowling of Bf 109D

10
11.(N)/JG 2
worn on the cowling of Bf 109D

11
12./JG 2
worn on the cowling of Bf 109G

12
I./JG 2
personal emblem of Hauptmann Helmut Wick

13
3./JG 2
personal emblem of Hauptmann Hennig Strümpell

14
3./JG 2
personal emblem of Oberfeldwebel Franz Jänisch

15
3./JG 2
personal emblem of Oberfeldwebel Josef Heinzeller

Shortly after the noses of its fighters were repainted, III./JG 2 transferred eastwards to the Pas de Calais. Oberleutnant Carl-Heinz Röders' 9. *Staffel*, pictured at Oye-Plage in September, display the unit's 'Gnat' badge on their new yellow cowlings

Luftflotte 3's bombers for about three weeks. During that time they were switched to bombing the Midlands by night. This freed *Jafü* 3's Bf 109s for temporary service with *Luftflotte 2* over south-east England and the Greater London area. As a consequence, the *Jagdgeschwader 'Richthofen'* was assigned alternative landing grounds in the Pas de Calais. The Beaumont-de-Roger units (*Stab*, I. and II. *Gruppen*) would operate out of Mardyck, while III./JG 2 forsook Octeville for the smaller Oye-Plage.

During their first ten days based on these two fields right on the coast between Dunkirk and Calais, JG 2 claimed close on 100 RAF fighters shot down. As the Battle neared its climax, a number of pilots added significantly to their scores in a series of bloody encounters over the fields of Kent and the approaches to London. Wick, Machold and Hahn all achieved eight kills in this period, whilst Rudorffer, Bertram and 'Ku-Vo' Votel each got seven.

One name almost lost amidst this welter of successes was that of Kurt Bühlingen. But the Hurricane claimed on 4 September by this recently-joined young unteroffizier was the first rung of a career which would see him rise to become the *Kommodore* of JG 2 for the last 12 months of the war.

The above victories, whether multiple or single, had not been achieved without cost, however. Nine pilots – perhaps no less able than their better known comrades, but certainly unluckier – failed to return across the narrow stretch of Channel separating England from France, for the Hurricanes and Spitfires were still fighting back, and hard.

The expected collapse of RAF Fighter Command had failed to materialise, and the initiative was beginning to slip from the Luftwaffe's grasp. In his Berchtesgaden retreat high in the Bavarian Alps, Adolf Hitler was already seeking a scapegoat to blame for his 'inability' to launch the long-delayed cross-Channel invasion.

Future *Geschwaderkommodore* Kurt Bühligen (centre) began his rise to fame with a Hurricane claimed over Kent on 4 September. He is seen here just over two months later with a rudder tally already standing at eight (the last a Spitfire shot down east of Portland on 10 November)

A propaganda shot using a captured Spitfire . . . or a wingman with nerves of steel calmly photographing his leader as he banks to attack an enemy fighter?

Oberst Harry von Bülow–Bothkamp takes leave of III./JG 2 pilots assembled in one of 8. *Staffel's* camouflaged dispersal pens at Oye-Plage

The obvious target for the Führer's wrath was Hermann Göring. But the only solution the portly *Reichsmarschall* could offer as a remedy for his fighters' 'lack of aggression' – a charge he had levelled during a stormy meeting with his unit commanders on 19 August – was to replace all those 'old men' still leading his frontline *Jagdgeschwader* with younger, more dynamic officers.

Having only recently been awarded the Knight's Cross for those very qualities he was now, in effect, being accused of lacking, Oberst Harry von Bülow-Bothkamp was one of the last to go. But on 2 September he, too, was finally 'kicked upstairs'. He took formal leave of each of his three *Gruppen* before departing to assume the first of a series of staff positions which would ultimately see him in command of 5. *Jagddivision* during the fateful days of the Defence of the Reich.

Von Bülow's leaving set in motion a series of command changes within the *Geschwader*. His immediate replacement at its head was III. *Gruppe's* Hauptmann Wolfgang Schellmann, *Legion Condor* veteran, contemporary of Galland and Mölders, and the archetypal officer Göring believed would restore his *Jagdwaffe's* standing. Schellmann's position as *Kommandeur* of II./JG 2 was taken by the very able, eight-victory Hauptmann Karl-Heinz Greisert.

The other two *Gruppen* also changed leadership before the month was out. On 7 September Major Hennig Strümpell was posted to Fighter School 4 at Fürth. And, once again, his moving paved the way for one of his subordinates to succeed him. The same officer who had stepped into his shoes when he relinquished command of 3. *Staffel* – Helmut Wick – was now appointed *Gruppenkommandeur* of I./JG 2. Finally, on 24 September, III. *Gruppe's* Major Dr Erich Mix, possibly the last World War 1 fighter pilot still operational, handed over the reins to Hauptmann Otto Bertram (the indefatigable Dr Mix, however, was subsequently to reappear on frontline duty as *Kommodore* of JG 1).

An informal photograph of Hauptmann Wolfgang Schellmann, *Gruppenkommandeur* of II./JG 2, before his promotion to major and appointment as *Geschwaderkommodore*

The month of September also saw the award of the *Geschwader's* next three Knight's Crosses. Oberfeldwebel Werner Machold and Oberleutnant Hans Hahn each received theirs for achieving the obligatory 20 kills. Wolfgang Schellmann, with 12 victories in Spain and another 10 since, was presumably honoured in part for his leadership of JG 2, whose I. *Gruppe* was currently recognised as the most successful in the entire Luftwaffe.

Göring little realised just how close he had come to attaining his objective. The Luftwaffe's recent raids on Fighter Command's sector airfields had been on the point of achieving what *'Adlertag'* had so signally failed to accomplish – the crippling of the RAF's defences – when Hitler suddenly ordered the bombers to attack London instead. It was this decision, taken in direct retaliation for the first bombs dropped on Berlin, which, many argue, was to cost the Luftwaffe the Battle.

JG 2's participation in the decisive turning point of the Battle in the south-east was minimal. During the latter half of September they claimed just four victories over the Home Counties, and suffered an equal number of casualties. Long before the month was out most of the *Geschwader* had returned to *Luftflotte 3* in the west.

Back over familiar territory – the 100-mile (160-km) stretch of open water between the Bay of the Seine and the Solent – they were soon making their presence felt again. On 26 September, while supporting a raid on the Supermarine works at Woolston, they shot down no fewer than 12 RAF fighters over the Southampton and Isle of Wight areas. Among the claimants on this date was that fledgling *Experte* Oberleutnant Bruno Stolle of 8. *Staffel*, whose victim may have been the No 152 Sqn Spitfire (this unit lost two aircraft during the engagement) which went into the sea 12 miles (19 km) south of the Needles.

Over the next week JG 2 went back to the same stretch of coastline between Portland and Selsey on four separate occasions, its pilots adding another two-dozen kills to their scoreboard in the process. But it was on 5 October, when two *Gruppen* of Ju 88 bombers were sent to attack Southampton, that the next major clash occurred. Flying cover, Helmut Wick's I. *Gruppe* reportedly downed 11 Hurricanes off Bournemouth.

Upon returning to Normandy towards the end of September, the *Geschwader* also used Querqueville as a forward strip. An ex-French land- and seaplane base right on the coast just outside Cherbourg (the Luftwaffe termed it Cherbourg-West), it was the take-off point for many of October's successful cross-Channel missions. Whether viewed from the air (with the beach at centre right) . . .

Wick himself claimed three, as did Oberfeldwebel Rudolf Täschner. At the time it was believed that they had wiped out an entire RAF squadron without loss to themselves.

Shortly after arriving back at base, Wick was summoned to the telephone. At the other end of the line was an effusive Göring, calling to congratulate the *Kommandeur* and his *Gruppe* on their success. The *Reichsmarschall* may have been a trifle less pleased had he known that the Hurricane squadron in question, Tangmere-based No 607, had, in fact, lost just one aircraft (P3554), whose pilot (Plt Off D Evans) had bailed out over Swanage uninjured. Three others forced-landed, but were subsequently repaired.

Helmut Wick returned to his favourite hunting ground south of the Isle of Wight that same day, where he was credited with two more Spitfires. These five kills in a single day had taken Wick's official score to 42. Twenty-four hours later, on 6 October, he was promoted to the rank of major and awarded the Oak Leaves to his Knight's Cross. He was only the fourth member of the Wehrmacht to receive this decoration (after Generalleutnant Eduard Dietl, the hero of Narvik, Mölders and Galland).

. . . or from the ground (with the sea in the background), Cherbourg-West was often a hive of activity

Exactly a fortnight after his promotion, Major Helmut Wick reached the pinnacle of his career. On 20 October Major Wolfgang Schellmann departed to assume command of JG 27, and Helmut Wick took over the leadership of JG 2 to become the youngest *Geschwaderkommodore* in the Luftwaffe. Wick's first order of the day in his new post is revealing;

'The *Herr Reichsmarschall* has conferred upon me the high honour of appointing me to be the head of the famous *Jagdgeschwader "Richthofen" No 2*. I have as of today assumed leadership of the *Geschwader*. I must express special thanks to my predecessor, Major Schellmann, for the splendid example he has set, not only in upholding the tradition of the *Geschwader*, but in adding to its fame and glory.

'I am fully aware of the duty and responsibility I am accepting, and undertake to lead the *Geschwader* in the same spirit of constant readiness you have all displayed in the past. I mean to be your leader by the example I set and the achievements I accomplish. At the same time I intend to be your truest comrade.'

Major Helmut Wick is seen wearing his newly-awarded Oak Leaves. This photograph clearly shows Wick's personal 'little bird' emblem ahead of the *Kommandeur's* double chevron on his densely-dappled *Emil*

Wick had already demonstrated that he was quite capable of looking after the interests of those under him. When still a lowly *Staffelkapitän*, his unit had been inspected by the GOC *Luftflotte 3*, *Generalfeldmarschall* Hugo Sperrle. When the latter suggested, as generals are wont to do, that the groundcrews could do with a little smartening up, Wick brusquely informed him that 'these men are working day and night to keep our fighters in the air, and have better things to do than to get their hair cut!'

Following Wick's promotion, I./JG 2's new *Kommandeur* was Hauptmann Karl-Heinz Krahl. Although he had not scored during his service as an NCO pilot with the *Legion Condor*, Krahl had since added a dozen kills to the Morane he had downed back in April.

Whether as a result of Wick's growing prestige or not is unclear, but JG 2 was the *Geschwader* chosen to stage southwards on 20 October to Mont de Marsan. Here, it was tasked with providing an aerial umbrella while Hitler met with the Spanish dictator General Franco at Hendaye on the border between occupied France and Spain. Upon its return to the Channel port six days later, III. *Gruppe* took up residence at Bernay, some seven miles (12 km) to the west of Beaumont-le-Roger – the smaller strip at Le Havre/Octeville had now been given over to the *Geschwader's* newly-established *Ergänzungsstaffel* (replacement training squadron).

The RAF was soon made aware that JG 2 was back in action after its brief stay in southern France, for on 27 October No 145 Sqn lost a pair of Hurricanes to 1. *Staffel* south-east of the Isle of Wight.

The following day *Reichsmarschall* Göring paid a visit to the *Geschwader*, and its dynamic new young *Kommodore* at his Cherbourg-West HQ. Pictures of the occasion were widely published in the national press and shown on German newsreels.

On that same 28 October Hauptmann Otto Bertram of III./JG 2, whose score was standing at 13, was awarded the Knight's Cross and ordered to return to Germany. This was no reflection on his abilities either as *Gruppenkommandeur* or operational pilot. 'Otsch' Bertram was one of three brothers serving in the Luftwaffe, two of whom had been lost – Hans, *Gruppen-Adjutant* of I./JG 27, had been shot down over Sussex the previous month, and now Karl, pilot of a Bf 110 nightfighter of 9./NJG 1, had been killed when he crashed west of Kiel following an engagement with a British bomber this very night.

In accordance with current Luftwaffe regulations, Otto, as the sole surviving brother, was immediately prohibited from further combat duty. He would spend the remainder of the war in various staff and training posts. Oberleutnant Hans Hahn – the irrepressible 'Assi', *Staffelkapitän* of 4./JG 2 – moved to Bernay to take command of III. *Gruppe*.

Throughout the last days of October and the first week of November – the official 'close' of the Battle according to many British historians – the *Jagdgeschwader 'Richthofen'* continued to take a heavy toll of RAF fighters along the length of Hampshire and Dorset coastline they had come to regard as their own.

Helmut Wick was intent on proving that his stated intention of leading by example was not just an empty phrase. His *Stabsschwarm* was at the

On 28 October Göring visited the *Geschwader* at Cherbourg-West. Here, he chats to a group of pilots, including Helmut Wick (in leather jacket to his left), Bruno Stolle (on his immediate right in kapok life-jacket) and Werner Machold (peaked cap). Another photograph taken of this group appeared on the front cover of a Berlin magazine exactly one month later, 28 November – the very day of Wick's disappearance

Seven days later, on 4 November, *Reichsmarschall* Göring was back with the *Jagdgeschwader 'Richthofen'* – this time on an official tour of inspection to Beaumont-le-Roger. Flanked by a more formally-attired Major Wick and the GOC *Luftflotte 3, Generalfeldmarschall* Hugo Sperrle (left), he reviews his troops

forefront in most of the action, and he and his two regular wingmen, Oberleutnants Erich Leie and Rudolf 'Rudi' Pflanz, claimed three Hurricanes and a Spitfire near Portsmouth in the mid-afternoon of 29 October. On 5 November it was another trio of Hurricanes, plus two Spitfires, north-east of Portland. The next day they accounted for four more Hurricanes and three Spitfires over the Solent, and 24 hours later still four Hurricanes south of Portsmouth.

Wick alone was credited with more than half of the above victories. A single Hurricane on 8 November took his total to 54. Although the *Kommodore* was undoubtedly the most successful, other *'Richthofen'* pilots continued to add to their scores too, as witness the Knight's Cross awarded on 9 November to 4. *Staffel's* Leutnant Siegfried Schnell for his 20th kill – one of three Hurricanes of No 145 Sqn shot down within seconds of each other south of the Isle of Wight two days earlier (the other two being claimed by Julius Meimberg and Kurt Bühlingen).

By the time of Göring's second visit, the Battle – from the enemy's point of view at least – was officially over. According to many British historians it had ended on 31 October, but try telling that to Oberleutnant Hermann Reifferscheidt, *Staffelkapitän* of 1./JG 2, who bellied in north of Selsey Bill on 1 November after being attacked by future Belgian ace Jean Offenberg of No 145 Sqn. The Hurricane pilot describes the action in the following quote from his wartime journal;

'. . . out of the blue a Me attacked us from the rear. I saw him too late in my mirror. He broke away underneath our formation and I dived immediately to find myself 400 yards behind, almost on his tail. I fired a burst which must have hit for he turned away seawards streaming glycol. A bit of the pilot's cockpit broke away and he dived. I followed him and gave him three more bursts which finished him.'

Note the signs of a previous identity (overpainted command chevrons) ahead of the white '9'

On 13 November the *Geschwader's* eighth and final Knight's Cross of 1940 was bestowed upon Hauptmann Karl-Heinz Krahl. Although his personal total was still five short of the mandatory twenty, his recent leadership of the high-scoring I. *Gruppe* was presumably a contributory factor.

Another milestone was reached on 16 November when JG 2 *'Richthofen'* officially achieved its 500th victory with Oberfeldwebel Willinger's destruction of a Hurricane over Portsmouth. Some sources record Willinger's kill, and the two others claimed by III. *Gruppe* within minutes of it, as being on 15 November. Unfortunately, RAF loss tables contain nothing to confirm either date.

There followed nearly a fortnight's pause – brought on as much by the exhaustion and strain being felt by the opposing sides, as by the worsening winter weather – with neither victories nor casualties to report. It was very much the calm before the storm . . . a storm of unimaginable proportions.

On the afternoon of 28 November Helmut Wick and his faithful *Stabsschwarm* were once again over the Isle of Wight. Wick, his wingman Erich Leie, and Unteroffizier Günther Seeger of 3. *Staffel* each claimed a Spitfire. The *Kommodore's* victory (possibly the aircraft flown by No 602 Sqn's Plt Off A Lyall, who was killed when he bailed out of the stricken fighter too late) took his total to 55, and made him the highest-scoring fighter pilot in the entire Luftwaffe. He had previously shared this accolade with JG 51's Werner Mölders, whose tally stood at 54 victories.

It was a position Wick would live to savour for less than two hours.

Arriving back at Cherbourg-Querqueville,.and determined to make the most of this rare spell of good weather (it was a perfect winter's day, with a clear blue sky and unlimited visibility), Wick immediately ordered the machines to be refuelled and re-armed, before setting off back across the Channel to the same area off the Solent – the scene of so many of his recent triumphs. And, once again, he spotted a formation of Spitfires climbing to intercept. The *Kommodore*, with Oberleutnant Erich Leise on his wing, dived to the attack, and within seconds Wick's 56th victim, a Spitfire of No 609 Sqn (R6631, flown by Plt Off P A Baillon, who was killed) was going down in flames.

If every picture is worth a thousand words, then the following three photographs (two overleaf) more than suffice to chart Helmut Wick's meteoric rise. Firstly, 'Yellow 2' sports the 22 kill bars of early September during his days as a *Knight's* Cross winner and *Staffelkapitän* of 3./JG 2 . . .

. . . by 6 October the yellow '2' had given way to *Kommandeur's* chevrons, and the rudder tally had grown to the 42 victories which won him the Oak Leaves and promotion to major . . .

It was to be his last success. Pulling out of the dive, Wick banked steeply and – for a split-second – flashed across the nose of another No 609 Sqn Spitfire. Instinctively, its pilot, reputedly Flt Lt John Dundas, himself a seven-victory Battle of Britain veteran (see *Osprey Aircraft of the Aces 12 - Spitfire Mk I/II Aces 1939-41* for further details), triggered his eight machine guns. The short but concentrated burst mortally damaged the heavily-mottled Messerschmitt. Wick managed to jettison his canopy and bail out, but the solitary parachute drifting down towards the sea to the south-west of the Needles was the last anybody ever saw of the Luftwaffe's leading ace.

John Dundas also disappeared, shot down into the sea off Bournemouth by 'Rudi' Pflanz a few moments later.

Despite intensive air and sea searches – Göring despatched E-boats to scour the area after darkness fell and even, it is reported, made use of the international distress wavelength to ask the British Air Ministry for news – no trace of Major Helmut Wick was ever found. His loss was officially announced on 4 December.

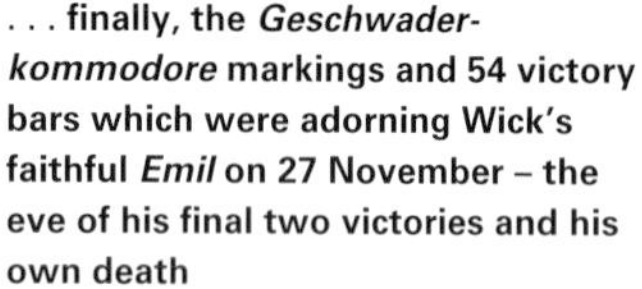

. . . finally, the *Geschwaderkommodore* markings and 54 victory bars which were adorning Wick's faithful *Emil* on 27 November – the eve of his final two victories and his own death

GUARDING THE RAMPARTS

Helmut Wick's disappearance marked the end of a chapter in the history of the *Jagdgeschwader 'Richthofen'*. It also effectively brought to a close the campaigns of 1940. JG 2 would claim just one more success and suffer one further fatality before the year was out. The No 59 Sqn Blenheim shot down into the Channel by 4. *Staffel's* 'Jule' Meimberg on the afternoon of 29 November went almost unheeded in the aftermath of the previous day's traumatic events. The sole casualty was an unfortunate NCO of the *Ergänzungsstaffel*, who crashed on a training flight near Octeville on 30 December.

But the loss of Helmut Wick heralded an even more fundamental change in the cross-Channel air war. Up until this time JG 2 had experienced nothing but success as they advanced from Berlin to the westernmost extremities of occupied France. Now that advance had been blunted.

On 20 December a pair of Spitfires strafed Le Touquet airfield. It was the first time UK-based Spitfires had operated over France since the completion of the Dunkirk evacuation in early June. Less than three weeks later, on 9 January 1941, three squadrons of Spitfires 'trailed their coats' at high altitude along the French coast. This was the start of RAF Fighter Command's new policy of 'leaning forward into France'.

JG 2 would fight fiercely to combat this new-found aggression on the part of their hitherto beleaguered opponents. But slowly the *Geschwader's* hard won dominance over 'their' stretch of England's southern coastline was eroded. In the weeks and months which lay ahead, as Fighter Com-

Hauptmann Wilhelm Balthasar was photographed shortly after assuming command of the *Geschwader* in February 1941. His tenure of office would last less than five months

mand grew progressively stronger – and the *Jagdwaffe* in the west became ever more thinly stretched – the aerial 'frontline' would move inexorably closer to JG 2's own home bases: from southern England, to mid-Channel, and thence into northern France.

At first, however, the winter of 1940-41 was used by both sides primarily as a welcome opportunity for rest and recuperation. Nothing illustrated this hiatus better than the failure to appoint an immediate successor to Helmut Wick. In the past, whenever a command position had fallen vacant it had been filled without delay. Now II. *Gruppe's* Karl-Heinz Greisert was named as acting *Kommodore* until further notice.

In common with most other *Geschwader* in the west, JG 2 also spent some time on home leave in Germany, where the pilots not only enjoyed an all-expenses-paid winter skiing holiday in the Alps, courtesy of their munificent *Reichsmarschall*, but were also introduced to the new Bf 109F (see *Osprey Aircraft of the Aces 29 - Bf 109F/G/K Aces of the Western Front* for further details). Although this latest addition to the Messerschmitt family was not yet coming off the production lines in sufficient numbers to allow all units to re-equip simultaneously, JG 2's *Staffeln* would take piecemeal delivery of their *Friedrichs* throughout the coming spring, and be fully converted in time to counter Fighter Command's renewed offensive in the summer.

The officer who had been selected to lead the *Geschwader* in this new phase of its operational career was of the highest calibre. Wilhelm Balthasar was another ex-*Legion Condor* ace, with seven Republican kills to his credit. He had emerged from the Battle of France as that campaign's top scorer, claiming 23 aerial victories, plus a further 13 aircraft destroyed on the ground. This feat won him the *Jagdwaffe's* second Knight's Cross (three weeks after Mölders) and promotion from *Staffelkapitän* of 7./JG 27 to *Gruppenkommandeur* of III./JG 3. Now fully recovered from wounds received during a dogfight with Spitfires over Canterbury on 4 September 1940, Hauptmann Balthasar assumed command of the *Jagdgeschwader 'Richthofen'* on 16 February 1941.

The spring of 1941 was to witness the complete re-organisation of the Luftwaffe's fighter forces along the Channel coast. With all plans for a seaborne invasion of England abandoned, the Führer's attention was now focused further afield – at first towards the south and south-east (the Mediterranean and the Balkans) and then eastwards on the Soviet Union.

One *Jagdgeschwader* after the other was withdrawn from the west to participate in these new campaigns until, finally, only the two senior-most remained – JG 2 *'Richthofen'*, and its 1936 progeny JG 26 *'Schlageter'*. Each was assigned a specific area of operations. JG 26 was to be responsible for the protection of the coastal provinces of Belgium and north-east France, while JG 2's bailiwick took in the whole of the French Channel coast west of the Seine to the Atlantic.

Although these zones remained in force throughout the next three years of increasingly bitter fighting, they were not inviolate. Each *Geschwader* could, and did, operate from its neighbour's territory whenever operational demands required it. Even within its own boundaries, such was the size of the area JG 2 was now defending that its component *Gruppen*, and even individual *Staffeln*, would often be forced to transfer from one airfield to another as circumstances dictated.

One of 9. *Staffel's* new Bf 109Fs displays the change of III. *Gruppe* marking from a 'wavy' to vertical bar. This particular machine, 'Yellow 8', would be lost on 2 July 1941 – just 24 hours before Balthasar's *Friedrich* spun in – when Feldwebel Heinz Jahner was forced to bail out wounded during a dogfight near St Omer

The first of these many redeployments had already been carried out in the spring of 1941. I. and III. *Gruppen* did not move far, the former taking temporary leave of Beaumont for their forward base at Cherbourg-Théville, and the latter vacating Bernay for nearby Caen-Roquancourt. By contrast, II. *Gruppe* was transferred to Brest, on the westernmost tip of the Brittany peninsula.

The reason for II./JG 2's transfer to Brest was the presence there of the battlecruisers *Scharnhorst* and *Gneisenau*. These 32,000-ton sister vessels had been at large in the Atlantic for almost seven weeks, sinking 22 Allied merchantmen. Hounded by British forces, the two ships had sought the illusory safety of the fortified French naval port, rather than risk the hazardous passage through the Denmark Strait, between Greenland and Iceland, back to home waters.

British reconnaissance aircraft located the battlecruisers on 28 March, six days after their arrival in Brest. The first RAF bombing raid took place two nights later. Over 60 further attacks, both by day and night, would be launched against the two ships over the course of the next 11 months.

II./JG 2's transfer to Brittany to strengthen the port's defences was to prove timely. One of the earliest daylight raids was mounted by 11 Hampdens on 1 April. Although the bombers reportedly turned back due to lack of cloud cover, one unfortunate was caught by 4. *Staffel's* Feldwebel Georg Bock and shot down some 12 miles (20 km) north of the target area. This No 144 Sqn machine was the *Jagdgeschwader 'Richthofen's'* first recorded kill of 1941 – less easy to identify are the three Blenheims claimed by II. *Gruppe* over Brittany five days later.

The areas in which three of the seven aircraft destroyed by the *Geschwader* during the latter half of April were brought down reveal just how wide-ranging – perhaps 'thinly spread' would be the more accurate – JG 2's operations were becoming. The three comprised a Spitfire claimed over the Straits of Dover by Werner Machold on 16 April, another Spitfire south of the Isle of Wight by Kurt Votel and a Blenheim off the Channel Islands by Erich Rudorffer.

The latter pair, both claimed on 21 April, also serve to illustrate the vagaries of fate which beset every frontline unit. 'Ku-Vo' Votel's Spitfire was his 12th, and final, victory. He was subsequently killed in a mid-air collision with Unteroffizier Hermann Maier over Théville on 3 May, whereas Rudorffer's Blenheim took his score to 20, earned him the Knight's Cross – awarded on 1 May – and set him firmly on the road to further successes.

Another claim made at the time, for a Spitfire brought down off Brighton by Feldwebel Helmut Schönemann on 18 April, was the first combat kill to be credited to the *Ergänzungsstaffel*. The training unit's score had climbed into double figures by the time it was detached from the *Geschwader* in the autumn, later to form part of *Ergänzungsjagdgruppe West*.

On the evening of 17 May *Kommodore* Wilhelm Balthasar achieved his first victory at the head of JG 2 – a No 54 Sqn Spitfire shot into the Channel between Dover and Calais. Forty-eight hours later he claimed his second – a Blenheim south of the Isle of Wight. Some hours earlier, shortly after midday on that same 19 May, a dogfight had taken place over traditional JG 2 territory off Portland. But the high-scoring, loss-free clashes of 1940 were a thing of the past, and although Werner Machold claimed a brace of Spitfires, three *Emils* of I. *Gruppe* failed to return. All three pilots did, however, survive.

In fact, encounters such as these off the south coast of England would soon become the exception rather than the rule. In the second week of June 1941 the RAF's self-styled 'non-stop' summer offensive really got underway. The 'lean' into France, which had begun as a two-aircraft trickle in December, quickly became a flood.

The British offensive was composed of specific types of operations, each with its own code-name. 'Rhubarbs' and 'Rodeos', for example, were purely fighter sweeps (differing only in the numbers involved) designed to draw the Bf 109s up into combat, but which the *Jagdwaffe* often chose to ignore as posing no threat. A 'Circus', on the other had, was built around a small force of bombers accompanied by a large fighter escort. These had the desired effect. Charged with the protection of key military and industrial targets in their assigned sectors, JGs 2 and 26 could not afford to let enemy bombers, however few in number, parade at will over areas they were responsible for defending.

This increased RAF pressure along the Channel coast resulted in another round of redeployment for the *Jagdgeschwader 'Richthofen'*. Hauptmann Greisert's II./JG 2 was recalled from Brest, where it was replaced by I. *Gruppe*, to Abbeville-Drucat. It did not remain here for long, however, and was soon on the move again, joining the *Geschwaderstab* and III./JG 2 (the latter arriving from Ligescourt) at St Pol-Bryas by the beginning of May.

The quickening tempo of operations over northern France during the latter half of June set the pattern for the coming summer months. The *Geschwader's* total score began to climb rapidly again, with 55 victories being claimed in just five days from 21 to 25 June. But losses were rising too.

On 17 June JG 2 had suffered its first recorded combat fatality with the new Bf 109F when III. *Gruppe's* Unteroffizier Heinz Seuffert was shot down into the sea west of Cherbourg. Less than a week later, on 23 June (a day the *Geschwader* claimed a dozen enemy aircraft destroyed, including a pair of Blenheims each to Balthasar and Siegfried Schnell), it lost four more *Friedrichs*, plus two others damaged. Although reports that 9./JG 2 was virtually wiped out on this date now appear to have been exaggerated, the *Staffel* had certainly been hit hard. Three of the four pilots killed were from its ranks, including eight-victory *Staffelkapitän* Oberleutnant Carl-Hans Röders.

Röders was the second *Staffelkapitän* lost to 'Assi' Hahn's III. *Gruppe* in the space of a fortnight. Although most of JG 2's actions were now perforce being fought on the French side of the Channel, a number of pilots were still attempting to take the war to the enemy's shore by flying 'tip-and-run' *Jabo* (fighter-bomber) raids along England's south coast.

The plan to adapt standard *Jagdgeschwader* for such operations had originated towards the close of the Battle of Britain, when losses among the Luftwaffe's *Kampfgruppen* were becoming prohibitive. Göring had decreed that a third of his *Jagdwaffe* should be converted to carry bombs. Each *Geschwader* was allowed to implement this order in its own way, and in JG 2's case it was decided that one *Staffel* from each *Gruppe* would be fitted with ventral bomb racks – although just how 1., 6. and 7. *Staffeln* came to be selected for this dubious honour is unclear.

Although *Jabo* missions were not to every pilot's liking, once their bombs had been dropped they were free to operate in true fighter mode. None had been more successful in this than the *Staffelkapitän* of 7./JG 2, Hauptmann Werner Machold. But the two Spitfires Machold had claimed near Weymouth on 19 May were to be his last. During a low-level raid over the same area on 9 June, anti-aircraft fire from the destroyer HMS *Blencathra* had damaged Machold's engine. It quickly seized and he had little option but to glide inland and seek a suitable spot for a belly landing. He found one west of Swanage, and sat out the rest of the war as a PoW.

During the late spring and early summer of 1941 Fighter Command's Spitfire IIs suffered badly at the hands of the *Friedrichs*, as witness this rather large 'trophy' in 9./JG 2's dispersal area. Note that the Bf 109Fs' yellow noses have now disappeared, as too has the *Geschwader* badge below the cockpit

JG 2 had thus lost its second Knight's Cross holder. Infinitely worse was soon to follow. Re-equipment with the Bf 109F meant that the *Geschwader* was more than holding its own against the RAF's new Spitfire Mk V (see *Osprey Aircraft of the Aces 16 - Spitfire Mk V Aces 1941-45* for further details), but the integrity of the *Friedrich's* aerodynamically refined airframe had long been suspect. And despite early problems with its tail unit having been resolved by the addition of external stiffeners, unexplained losses continued to occur. Then, on 28 June, the wing of a JG 26 machine collapsed during a dogfight, killing 31-victory *Experte* Oberleutnant Gustav Sprick.

Four days later JG 2 was celebrating the award of the Oak Leaves to their *Kommodore* for his achieving 40 confirmed kills. But the very next afternoon, at 1525 hours on 3 July, Hauptmann Wilhelm Balthasar was to lose his life in almost identical circumstances to 'Micky' Sprick. The wing of his F-4 reportedly sheared off when he attempted an evasive spiral dive manoeuvre during combat with a group of Spitfires. Balthasar was unable to escape from the wildly spinning machine, and his body was recovered from the wreckage of the aircraft, which had crashed to earth on the edge of Aire-Wittes, a small hamlet south-east of St Omer.

Posthumously promoted to major, Wilhelm Balthasar was laid to rest in a World War 1 cemetery in Flanders alongside his father, who had fallen in that earlier conflict.

Despite the loss of Balthasar, there was no let-up for the pilots of II. and III. *Gruppen* as the RAF continued to exert maximum pressure from across the Channel. Casualties were becoming more frequent, but they were still far outstripped by JG 2's lengthening list of kills. 'Assi' Hahn's III./JG 2 was particularly successful during this period of intense activity. The *Kommandeur's* own total was also mounting steadily. But the score rate of two of his *Staffelkapitäne* – Egon Mayer, who had replaced Werner Machold at the head of 7./JG 2, and Siegfried Schnell of 9./JG 2 – was little short of spectacular.

It was largely thanks to *Experten* such as these that the OKW was able to announce on 8 July that the *Jagdgeschwader 'Richthofen'* had reached a total of 644 aerial victories, thereby equalling the record set by its World War 1 namesake.

Of the twelve RAF aircraft brought down on that date, five had been credited to Mayer and three to Schnell. Twenty-four hours later Mayer claimed just one, but Schnell downed another trio on each of two separate missions. Nine Spitfires in two days! With his total having thus risen from 35 to 44, 'Wumm' Schnell was immediately awarded the Oak Leaves.

A number of other pilots – some, familiar names, others less so – scored multiple kills over the course of the next fortnight. But on 23 July JG 2's still leaderless *Stabsschwarm* had a veritable field day over the Pas de Calais. Between them they accounted for now fewer than 15 RAF fighters, Oberleutnants Erich Leie and Rudolf Pflanz each claiming six and Oberfeldwebel Günther Seeger being responsible for the remaining three. A further 16 enemy aircraft were claimed by the remainder of the *Geschwader*. Actual RAF losses due to enemy action amounted to 11 Spitfires.

Among those in action was I. *Gruppe*, whose occupancy of Brest-Guipavas had been very quiet of late in comparison with the furious clashes currently raging along the Channel to the east. Although 1. *Staffel*

Scores may have been rising during the summer of 1941, but the strain was beginning to tell. This serious-looking pilot is Oberleutnant Siegfried Schnell, *Staffelkapitän* of 9./JG 2. He was credited with destroying nine Spitfires in two days early in July

was credited with only two of the day's 31 successes, its contribution was significant, for Leutnant Ulrich Adrian's victim, identified as a Stirling attacked over La Pallice, was almost certainly 'R-Robert' of No 15 Sqn. This aircraft is believed to have been the first four-engined enemy bomber destroyed by JG 2.

The pair of 'Boeing bombers' claimed by two pilots of 3. *Staffel* were also presumably other Stirlings of the six-strong formation that attacked La Pallice, but which returned to base safe, if not unscathed.

The sudden discovery by the RAF that *Scharnhorst* had temporarily vacated Brest for La Pallice, more than 200 miles (320 km) to the south, meant a hasty change to the long-planned major bombing raid scheduled for the following day. Instead of some 150 bombers concentrating on Brest alone, 79 Wellingtons and 18 Hampdens would now attack Brest, while a force of 15 Halifaxes targeted La Pallice.

Four weeks after Balthasar's loss, Walter Oesau arrived from the eastern front to take command of JG 2

With only the Hampdens enjoying the benefit of a fighter escort, the bombers approached the two ports in the early afternoon of 24 July. Visibility was clear, 'German fighter opposition was stronger and more prolonged than expected', and the result was inevitable.

The pilots of Hauptmann Krahl's I. *Gruppe* more than made up for their relative inactivity of recent weeks, for in the space of 90 minutes they claimed 18 bombers – and these claims tally remarkably closely with admitted RAF losses. From the Brest force ten Wellingtons did indeed fail to return, although only two of the three Hampdens credited were actually shot down. A third of the Halifaxes despatched against La Pallace were lost, four bombers being were correctly identified and claimed as such. The fifth was almost certainly the 'Stirling' downed by Unteroffizier Schmalenberg, whose aim appears to have been better than his aircraft recognition.

But the battle was far from one-sided, for eight of the *Gruppe's Emils* were lost and two others damaged. Six pilots were reported killed or missing, plus two wounded. At least three of the casualties had apparently engaged the Hampden force, for Feldwebel Erwin Richey and Unteroffizier Friedrich Schumann were each credited with one of these bombers, and Unteroffizier Walter Vock with a Spitfire, before all three were shot down and killed.

One of the two wounded was Leutnant Julius Meimberg, *Staffelkapitän* of 3./JG 2, who crash-landed after bringing down both a Hampden and a

Wellington. Three other pilots claimed doubles that day, including *Kommandeur* Karl-Heinz Krahl. One of his victims was another Spitfire, the *Gruppe* claiming a total of three RAF fighters. Two No 152 Sqn machines are listed as missing on this date, Spitfire Mk IIA P7881, piloted by 11-kill Battle of Britain ace Flg Off Eric 'Boy' Marrs DFC, having been shot down near Brest (RAF reports claim he was lost to flak).

With 86 victories of his own, one of the new *Geschwaderkommodore's* first duties was to host a press day in honour of three of his pilots' each being awarded the Knight's Cross for achieving 20 kills. Seen posing together for an official photograph are, from left to right, Olt Rudolf Pflanz (*Geschwader-TO*), Olt Erich Leie (*Geschwader-Adjutant*), Oesau and Lt Egon Mayer (*Staffelkapitän* 7./JG 2)

While I./JG 2 were battling RAF bombers over the Atlantic coast, the officer who had earlier replaced Wilhelm Balthasar at the head of III./JG 3 had just scored his 86th kill some 1700 miles (2700 km) to the east. Already wearing the Swords and Oak Leaves, Hauptmann Walter Oesau was now to be recalled from the eastern front to assume Balthasar's mantle for a second time – as *Geschwaderkommodore* of JG 2 *'Richthofen'*.

He took command on 29 July, introducing himself with the words;

'In the spirit of Manfred von Richthofen, and following the example set by my predecessors, Major Wick and Hauptmann Balthasar, constant readiness and devotion to duty will enable us to achieve yet further successes.'

To assist him in his new role, Oesau was fortunate to have inherited arguably the most experienced and successful *Stabsschwarm* of the Luftwaffe. Erich Leie and Rudolf Pflanz had flown alongside both the *Kommodores* named by Oesau above. And on 1 August each was awarded the Knight's Cross for reaching the 20-victory mark. Egon Mayer, *Staffelka-*

Another shot taken on the press day. Donning life-jackets, the quartet stage an informal 'walk-past' of one of the *Stabsschwarm* machines for the benefit of the photographer

As *Kommodore*, Major Oesau had two *Friedrichs* at his disposal. Although bearing the same combination of chevron and horizontal bar markings, they were not absolutely identical – note the application of the chevrons, for example

pitän of 7./JG 2, was also honoured on the same day, and for the same achievement. The triple celebration was officially recorded on film.

The third present member of the *Stabsschwarm*, Günther Seeger, whose score was currently standing at 13, would also receive the Knight's Cross, but not until 1944 – by which time he had been commissioned, was serving with JG 53 and had achieved 46 kills!

After a somewhat shaky start, as evidenced by this terse entry in his diary within a few days of his arrival, 'Got badly mauled today', Major Oesau scored his first victory with JG 2 on 10 August. Forty-eight hours later he was credited with four of the 15 Spitfires (and one Hurricane) claimed by the *Geschwader* – six Spitfires were actually lost. Three other Spitfires downed over the Pas de Calais area on that 12 August had fallen to the *Gruppenkommandeur* of III./JG 2. These took 'Assi' Hahn's score to 46, and earned him the Oak Leaves to his Knight's Cross.

19 August's 15 kills (14 actually lost) included ten more Spitfires in the same area between Dunkirk and Calais. This spate of victories had boosted the *Geschwader's* overall total past the 800 mark, but in the week which separated these two major fighter engagements, a solitary bomber claimed by I. *Gruppe* over Brest was to contribute another milestone to the history of JG 2.

On the morning of 16 August two Fortress Is of No 90 Sqn had taken off from Polebrook, in Northamptonshire, for yet another raid on the two battlecruisers. This time the attackers were relying on altitude for protection. But at 32,000 ft (9720 m) above the target area, in the highest interception of the war to date, they were set upon by fighters of I./JG 2. Although 1. *Staffel's* Stabsfeldwebel Erwin Kley was credited with the destruction of one of the Boeings, his victim ('D-Dog') managed to limp back to England. In attempting to crash-land at an airfield in Devon, however, the Boeing overshot, caught fire and was destroyed.

A replacement 'D-Dog', shot down over Norway on 8 September while en route to attack the pocket-battleship *Admiral Scheer*, would be the first Fortress to fall to direct enemy action. But Kley's brush with AN523 was JG 2's earliest recorded contact with the four-engined bomber, which, in different markings, was soon to become a very familiar foe.

The mid-August confrontations over the Straits of Dover with the fighter escorts of Circuses 81-84 were to prove the high-water mark of the *Geschwader's* 1941 campaigning. On only three further occasions during the remainder of the year would their daily total of victories creep into double figures. But individual scores still rose steadily, if no longer so steeply, as the *Friedrich* – in the hands of *Experten* now enjoying the twin benefits of operating over 'friendly' territory, and being able to choose where and when to engage their enemy – continued to display its superiority over the Spitfire V.

On 4 September two further Knight's Crosses were awarded to members of JG 2. Both were experienced Oberfeldwebel who had exceeded the 20-kill yardstick – 'old hand' Kurt Bühligen and a newcomer recently arrived from JG 53, Josef 'Sepp' Wurmheller. That same 4 September also saw another new type added to JG 2's growing list of victims when 9. *Staffel's* Unteroffizier Karl Nowak shot a twin-engined Whirlwind of No 263 Sqn (flown by Sgt G L Buckwell) into the Channel north of Cherbourg.

Nearly a fortnight's lull was to follow. But action flared up again during the latter half of the month when the *Geschwader's* score-sheet was made up entirely of Spitfires – 41 in all – for the single loss of 4./JG 2's Unteroffizier Heinz Hoppe, who succumbed during a dogfight near Abbeville on 20 September.

The unbroken list of Spitfire claims continued throughout October, leavened only by one (unidentified) Wellington credited to another 4. *Staffel* pilot, Leutnant Theo Eicher, on 15th. Of October's 33 Spitfires, nine had been downed by Oesau's *Stabsschwarm*. It was one of these, claimed in the early afternoon of 26 October, which gave the *Kommodore* his 100th kill. Walter Oesau thereby became only the third fighter pilot in history to achieve the century.

On 8 November the RAF's hard-fought 'non-stop' offensive finally ground to a halt following another costly operation – Circus 110 – which had been targeted at Lille. Fighter Command lost 17 Spitfires on that day, JG 2 claiming ten. Thereafter, although RAF fighters continued to mount cross-Channel sweeps in spite of the deteriorating weather, there was a dramatic easing of pressure.

The remainder of the month saw just one further kill and one operational fatality. Both occurred in the ranks of III./JG 2 which, as a conse-

On 26 October 1941 the *Stabsschwarm* claimed a trio of Spitfires, two falling to 'Rudi' Pflanz, and the third to the *Kommodore*. It was Oesau's 14th victory since his arrival on the Channel front three months earlier, and it also took him to the century mark – and cause for suitable celebration!

quence of the reduced activity over the Pas de Calais, had vacated Le Touquet, St Pol and the other fields it had been using in that region, and returned to Cherbourg-Théville on 17 November. Five days later 9. *Staffel's* Leutnant Werner Ahrendt was shot down in error by 'friendly' naval flak. And on 24 November Oberleutnant Bruno Stolle, *Staffelkapitän* of 8./JG 2, claimed a solitary Spitfire.

Meanwhile, changes had been taking place in I. *Gruppe* at Brest. *Kommandeur* Hauptmann Karl-Heinz Krahl had departed on 20 November to assume command of II./JG 3 in the Mediterranean, and his place was taken by Hauptmann Ignaz Prestele, a 13-victory *Experte*, and hitherto *Staffelkapitän* of 2./JG 53 on the eastern front.

And it was Prestele's I. *Gruppe* which bore the brunt of what little action there was in December. Two Hampdens downed late on the afternoon of 13 December by Leutnant Horst Walbeck and Feldwebel Kurt Meyer were undoubtedly the two machines of that type which failed to return from 'Gardening' (mine-laying) sorties off Brest on that date.

Walbeck was also among the eight claimants on 18 December when another heavy bombing raid was launched against the German warships in Brest harbour. As well as Walbeck's Manchester (of No 97 Sqn), I./JG 2 was credited with four Stirlings and three of the attacker's escorting fighters.

The following week I./JG 2 transferred to Morlaix, making way for the *Geschwaderstab* and Hauptmann Greisert's II. *Gruppe* to take up residence in Brest.

It thus fell to these latter units to counter the last bombing raid on Brest of 1941, and to score the *Geschwader's* final four kills of the year while so doing. The three Halifaxes claimed – one by the *Stabsschwarm's* Erich Leie – tally exactly with admitted RAF losses. Strangely, however, only Leutnant Fritz Maly of 5./JG 2 was credited with a Spitfire, whereas three of the fighter escort were reported lost in combat with Bf 109s off Brest by fellow RAF pilots.

The relative calm of the new year – the entire *Geschwader* claimed just five kills and suffered a single accidental injury in January 1942 – was illusionary. A major operation was brewing. Despite their concerted efforts,

RAF Bomber and Coastal Commands had so far failed to seriously damage the two battlecruisers (now joined by the heavy cruiser *Prinz Eugen*) holed up in Brest. But it could only be a matter of time.

With this in mind, and anxious to create a 'fleet-in-being' in Norwegian waters to help defend what he perceived to be his unprotected northern flank, Hitler had issued orders that the three capital ships were to be brought back from France. However, rather than risk the lengthy voyage north about the British Isles directly to Norway, he decreed that the flotilla should stage via Germany by an even more hazardous (some said suicidal) route – by making a high speed 'dash' along the English Channel and through the 21-mile (33-km) bottleneck of the Straits of Dover.

Such a gamble would depend not only on the element of surprise, but also on effective and continuous air cover. The Führer instructed his newly appointed *Inspekteur der Jagdflieger*, Oberst Adolf Galland, to provide just that. The latter's plan hinged upon the establishment of three major fighter sectors along the intended route of the 'dash', each responsible in turn for the protection of the flotilla as it progressed through their area.

JG 2 was the westernmost of the three main *Jagdgeschwader* involved in the operation. From its bases in Brittany and Normandy its pilots would escort the flotilla during the first part of its voyage along the Channel, before handing over to neighbouring JG 26 off the Pas de Calais. The point of overlap, and period of greatest combined strength, would thus coincide with the area of greatest danger as the vessels entered the Straits.

Just before 2300 hours on 11 February the three capital ships, and their escorting destroyers, slipped unnoticed out of Brest harbour. Operation *Cerberus* (the naval side of the operation) was underway. At first light next

A pair of *Friedrichs* fly low overhead as the Brest flotilla – *Scharnhorst* in the lead – plough their way line-ahead up the Channel

morning Operation *Donnerkeil* (*Thunderbolt*) – the Luftwaffe's code-name for its part in the combined undertaking – commenced as the first of the day's air patrols rendezvoused with the flotilla off Cherbourg.

Circling at low level beneath the 1650-ft (500-m) cloud base to avoid being picked up by British radar, and maintaining strict radio silence all the while, successive waves of JG 2's fighters – each 16-aircraft strong – maintained a series of 30-minute vigils over the ships as they ploughed eastwards through increasingly heavy rain and snow showers.

The atrocious weather conditions conspired with an incredible sequence of mishaps – and downright blunders – to prevent the British from detecting the ships' passage for close on 14 hours! And it was not until 1334 hrs on 12 February, as the flotilla was nearing Cap Gris Nez, that the first enemy aircraft in the shape of six antiquated Fairey Swordfish torpedo-bombers of the Fleet Air Arm's 825 Naval Air Squadron, accompanied by ten RAF Spitfires, were reported approaching.

But even as the 16 British machines bore down on the ships from the direction of the Kent coast, another formation of aircraft was spotted off to starboard. For a moment it appeared as if the flotilla was to be hit from both sides simultaneously, but the newcomers quickly revealed themselves to be Fw 190s of JG 26. The vulnerable torpedo biplanes could not have chosen a worse moment to launch their attack. Messerschmitts and Focke-Wulfs alike jostled for position, and within four minutes every one of the six Swordfish had been blown out of the sky.

After the long hours of nervous tension, all was confusion in this sudden explosion of action. Five pilots of JG 2 each claimed a Swordfish destroyed, as too did three of JG 26. The ships' flak gunners were later credited with a further ten!

Although the vessels were now entering JG 26's area of control, elements of JG 2 leapfrogged eastwards to continue the fight. As the flotilla hugged the Belgian and Dutch coasts further British strikes were mounted. They were to no avail, for the three ships would reach the haven of home waters without taking a single bomb or torpedo hit. But before darkness fell JG 2's additional claims included three Spitfires (two to 'Rudi' Pflanz) and a pair of Whirlwinds. Their final victims of the day were three Hampdens brought down off Holland, one each falling to Ignaz Prestele, Siegfried Schnell and Bruno Stolle.

The now historic 'Channel Dash' marked another watershed in the annals of the *Geschwader*, for a subtle change of emphasis would begin to be felt in the months ahead. Although there were many individual and group successes still to come, scores were no longer rising so sharply. And casualty lists were beginning to lengthen.

This is well illustrated by comparing 1941's seeming plethora of awards with 1942, when just two Knight's Crosses would be presented to the *Geschwader* – one posthumously, and neither to a high-scoring *Experte*. Instead, both would go to leaders of JG 2's specialised fighter-bomber *Staffel*, for the somewhat ad hoc *Jabo* operations first introduced towards the close of the Battle of Britain had since been reorganised on a more regular basis.

Both Channel-based *Jagdgeschwader* had been ordered to set up a specialist fighter-bomber unit, 13.(*Jabo*)/JG 2 being commanded by Oberleutnant Frank Liesendahl, formerly *Staffelkapitän* of 6./JG 2. Eschewing

As one of the first Fw 190As delivered to III. *Gruppe,* 'White 11' still carries the now decidedly anachronistic 'Chamberlain's hat' badge of 7. *Staffel*

their predecessors' predominantly high-altitude hit-and-run tactics, the pilots of 10.(*Jabo*) *Staffel* flew low-level attacks on Channel shipping and against shore installations along England's south coast.

Although they were to prove highly successful in this role – in its first three months of operations, between March and June 1942, the *Staffel* claimed the sinking of 20 vessels, totalling some 63,000 BRT – 10.(*Jabo*)/JG 2's activities were a mere pinprick when set against the RAF's renewed offensive over north-west Europe, which also got underway in March.

To its earlier repertoire of operations, the RAF now added 'Ramrods', 'Rangers' and 'Roadsteads'. The first two of these were improved 'Circus'-type missions – formations of bombers with strong fighter escort. The latter were aimed specifically at German shipping along the Channel and North Sea coasts.

To help it combat this increased pressure, the *Jagdgeschwader 'Richthofen'*, following in the footsteps of JG 26, also began to re-equip with the Focke-Wulf Fw 190 (see *Osprey Aircraft of the Aces 9 - Focke-Wulf Fw 190 Aces of the Western Front* for further details). Early in March, Hauptmann Prestele's I. *Gruppe* was ordered to send a small *Umrüstungskommando* (conversion detachment) to Le Bourget for retraining on the new radial-engined fighter. While there, the *Kommando* suffered a number of accidents, including JG 2's first Fw 190 fatality – Fritz Maly was killed when his engine burst into flames shortly after take-off (an unpleasant habit of early-production Fw 190s).

Thereafter, the *Geschwader* completed re-equipment on approximately a *Gruppe*-per-month basis. Come mid-March 'Assi' Hahn's III./JG 2 was already operational on interim Fw 190A-1s at Cherbourg-Théville and Morlaix, and by the latter half of April II. *Gruppe,* under Karl-Heinz Greisert, deployed A-2s at Beaumont-le-Roger and Triqueville. A month

Major Oesau arrives at 'Heino' Greisert's alfresco 34th birthday party, held on 2 February 1942. *Gruppenkommandeur* Greisert's Fw 190 provides the backdrop . . .

after that I./JG 2 would also have A-2s dispersed alongside its Bf 109Fs at Cherbourg, St Brieuc and Morlaix.

Initially, the *Geschwaderstab* opted to retain its trusty *Friedrichs*. Walter Oesau's 'century' back in October had automatically brought with it a ban on further combat flying (the rule at that time being that such national heroes had to be safeguarded from further danger). The *Stabsschwarm* had since been led by *Geschwader-Adjutant* Erich Leie, with Technical Officer (TO) 'Rudi' Pflanz and two new wingmen, Feldwebel Fritz Stritzel and Josef 'Jupp' Bigge, making up the quartet. The *Schwarm* had been increased to six machines by the end of 1941, with the addition of Leutnant Fritz Edelmann and Oberfeldwebel Carl.

. . . but a close-up of the birthday boy himself shows that II./JG 2 had not yet relinquished its last *Friedrichs* (left)

Springtime at Beaumont-le-Roger. Walter Oesau and Egon Mayer chat as they stroll along the perimeter track past one of the earth and timber blast walls erected to protect the aircraft . . .

. . . then it's time for the *Kommodore* to get a little office work done . . .

. . . before snatching 40 winks under the shade of the blossoming apple trees – note the airman, top left, on the fortified, elevated walkway which completely encircled the ground floor of the Ops HQ building

But all thoughts of a ban were dashed from Walter Oesau's mind on 17 April when the late afternoon calm at Beaumont-le-Roger was shattered by half-a-dozen four-engined bombers roaring low overhead. Otto Happel of the HQ signals section remembered the occasion vividly;

'Our fighters had been up on their final mission of the day. The first of them were just returning and preparing to land when somebody yelled, "*Viermots* flying low over the field!"

'I immediately warned our incoming fighters over the R/T of the danger. Major Oesau shot past me like greased lighting, heading straight for his Me 109, which was always kept at instant readiness. Without further ado he set off after the departing bombers.'

These bombers were the leading wave of 12 of the RAF's new Lancasters which had been sent on a daring, low-level daylight raid on the MAN diesel engine workshops at Augsburg, deep in Bavaria.

Oesau, presumably accompanied by Fritz Edelmann, who was slightly wounded in the ensuing action, soon caught up with the Lancasters, which were already under attack by II. *Gruppe's* Fw 190s. A long, running fight – lasting a full hour – resulted in four of the No 44 Sqn machines going down. Three had fallen to the Focke-Wulfs, *Kommandeur* Karl-Heinz Greisert claiming the first, followed by Feldwebel Bosseckert and Unteroffizier Pohl. Otto Happel again;

'We later learned that four of the bombers had been shot down. Pohl's victim was the *Geschwader's* 1000th kill, and Major Oesau's the 1001st!'

The latter aircraft, Lancaster Mk I L7536/KM-H, was only the tenth production Avro heavy bomber to be built. It had come down a few miles east of Evreux, and had taken Oesau's own score to 101. Back to Otto;

'It was common knowledge that *Kommodore* Oesau had received *Startverbot* (i.e. was banned from operational flying), but his excuse was a classic. He immediately informed his superiors that he had been up on a routine test flight when these monsters suddenly appeared from out of nowhere, and he had been forced to shoot down a Lancaster purely out of self-defence.'

JG 2's 1000 kills were officially broken down as follows;

Stabsschwarm	113
I. *Gruppe*	346
II. *Gruppe*	267
III. *Gruppe*	258
E.St./E.Gr.	16

Oesau's relaxation was shattered on 17 April when six Lancasters roared low over Beaumont on a daring daylight raid into Germany. This is reportedly the wreckage of one of them, but whether it is Pohl's or Oesau's victim is uncertain

The advent of the Fw 190 had come as a nasty surprise to RAF Fighter Command. But the shock of the unknown was dispelled by one of the greatest intelligence 'gifts' of the European air war when Oberleutnant Arnim Faber, the *Gruppen-Adjutant* of 'Assi' Hahn's III./JG 2 landed his almost brand-new A-3 by mistake in south Wales!

The first week in May witnessed two command changes. Karl-Heinz 'Heino' Greisert departed for a staff posting, the reins of II./JG 2 passing into the capable hands of the long-serving *Kapitän* of his 5. *Staffel*, Hauptmann Helmut Bolz. And just three days later, on 4 May, I. *Gruppe's* Hauptmann Ignaz Prestele was shot down in a dogfight north of Octeville. His place was taken by *Geschwader-Adjutant* Oberleutnant Erich Leie.

Leie's assuming the leadership of I./JG 2 marked the beginning of the end of the famous *'Richthofen' Stabsschwarm*, which by now was operating out of Ligescourt and flying high-cover intercept missions in conjunction with 1. *Staffel*. In mid-May part of 1./JG 2 was pulled out to re-equip with the first of the new Bf 109G series, the pressurised G-1. Once conversion was complete, this unit then became 11./JG 2 – the *Geschwader's* official high-altitude *Staffel*, command being given to the ex-TO, Oberleutnant Rudolf Pflanz.

The rump 1./JG 2 was also brought back up to strength, in part by incorporating the remainder of the now disbanded *Stabsschwarm*.

JG 2's new Fw 190s had come as a nasty shock to RAF Spitfire V pilots, who felt they were just beginning to get the edge over the *Geschwader's Friedrichs* during their sweeps over northern France. Now they were suddenly very much the underdogs once again (and would remain so until the advent of the superb 'stop-gap' Spitfire IX in July). In the interim, JG 2 made the most of its few weeks' undisputed technical superiority.

During one brief six-day period alone, from 30 May to 4 June, the *Geschwader* recaptured some of its former glory by claiming no fewer than 50 victories. Not surprisingly, many familiar names were involved. Siegfried Schnell's four kills in the space of ten minutes on 3 June took his total to 61, whilst others who scored doubles included Egon Mayer, Erich Rudorffer and Josef Wurmheller. Now operating separately, Erich Leie and Rudolf Pflanz each got one apiece (their 48th and 44th respectively).

'Rudi' Pflanz would claim just eight more kills. Number 51 went down on 30 July. Twenty-four hours later 11. *Staffel* was back aloft high above Abbeville as the next RAF raid came in. References differ as to exactly how

Siegfried Schnell's four victories on 3 June had taken his total to 61. With those safely 'booked' on his rudder scoreboard, his groundcrew now appear to be adding the finishing touches to number 62

The rudder of 'Assi' Hahn's equally immaculate 'White Double Chevron' also displays 61 kill bars, just seven short of the 68 he would achieve before leaving for the eastern front

Oberleutnant Frank Liesendahl (pictured, right, with Oesau), who had commanded 6. *Staffel* until his wounding in July 1941, was the first *Staffelkapitän* of 10.(*Jabo*)/JG 2, the specialist anti-shipping unit

Pflanz met his end, although it seems clear that he was unaware that he had become separated from his wingman, Feldwebel Heinz Grüber, and that his tail was unprotected as he attacked and destroyed his last Spitfire.

Seconds later his own machine was mortally hit. One report states that the *Gustav* 'exploded in mid-air', whilst another describes Pflanz as being unable to release the damaged canopy of the machine's pressurised cockpit. The wreckage impacted in the sand dunes south of Berck-sur-Mer.

Pflanz was not the only highly-experienced *Staffelkapitän* lost that month, for exactly a fortnight earlier, on 17 July, Oberleutnant Frank Liesendahl, leader of 10.(*Jabo*)/JG 2, had been killed by anti-aircraft fire while attacking a freighter off Brixham harbour in Devon. It was Liesendahl who, on 4 September, was awarded the *Jagdgeschwader 'Richthofen's'* only posthumous Knight's Cross.

August's actions were dominated by the ill-fated Allied landing attempt at Dieppe. While the Canadian regiments faced insuperable odds on the shingle beaches, the skies overhead were the scene of an equally bitter confrontation. The RAF lost almost exactly 100 aircraft on that 19 August, plus many more damaged. Nearly all were claimed by the fighters of JGs 2 and 26.

'Richthofen' pilots were credited with a staggering 59 confirmed kills and a further seven probables, and once again a host of well-known names are included among those claiming success. Erich Leie and Kurt Bühligen each got a Spitfire, while many others scored doubles, including Erich Rudorffer, Egon Mayer and 'Assi' Hahn (bringing their scores to 45, 50 and 67 respectively). 'Jule' Meimberg, who had taken over the high-altitude 11. *Staffel* after the death of Rudolf Pflanz, also downed two Spitfires. Günther Seeger went one better with three, and Siegfried Schnell better still with five (which took this total to 70).

But the outstanding performance of the day was undoubtedly that of 9. *Staffel's* Oberfeldwebel Josef Wurmheller, who added six Spitfires and a Blenheim (more likely a Baltimore) to his existing score of 54 – all while flying with a foot in plaster and suffering from suspected concussion! This feat would help earn 'Sepp' Wurmheller promotion to leutnant, and the Oak Leaves to his Knight's Cross.

On the other side of the coin JG 2 lost 11 Fw 190s and another ten machines damaged. Eight pilots were reported killed or missing, with a

'Sepp' Wurmheller demonstrates the kind of tactics that would bring him seven victories over Dieppe on 19 August, promotion to leutnant, and the Oak Leaves to that half-hidden Knight's Cross

The sun throws long shadows as quiet descends upon 7. *Staffel's* dispersal area after a hard day's work. A solitary pilot stands, seemingly lost in thought, in the middle of the taxyway as an armed sentry keeps watch nearby

further six wounded. Among those killed was 11. *Staffel's* Stabsfeldwebel Erwin Kley, whose *Gustav* overturned on landing at Le Tréport.

10.(*Jabo*)/JG 2 also had two Fw 190s damaged in landing accidents. The fighter-bomber *Staffel*, which had converted to the Focke-Wulf shortly before the death of Frank Liesendahl, and was now commanded by Oberleutnant Fritz Schröter, had focused its attention throughout the day on the shipping off the beaches. By its close they had damaged four landing craft and sunk two. They also claimed hits on two RN destroyers, with one – the *Berkeley* – being so badly damaged that she, too, had to be sunk.

For his leadership of the *Jabostaffel* in this, and other actions, Fritz Schröter would be awarded the Knight's Cross on 24 September.

Overshadowed by the mayhem around Dieppe, a diversionary raid by 22 high-flying four-engined bombers on Abbeville-Drucat airfield went almost unnoticed. But this mission, only the second by B-17 Flying Fortresses of the embryonic US Eighth Air Force, was just the beginning of a daylight bombing offensive which would ultimately reach into every corner of western Europe and beyond (see *Osprey Combat Aircraft 18 - B-17 Flying Fortress units of the Eighth Air Force* for further details).

At first, however, the pioneers of the 'Mighty Eighth' were still feeling their way, and restricting themselves to short cross-Channel raids into northern France and the Low Countries. This was territory defended by JG 26, and although 'Assi' Hahn led two *Staffeln* of his III. *Gruppe* into Poix, south of Abbeville, early in September to help stiffen the area's defences, it would be several weeks – and some 260 miles (420 km) distant – before *the Jagdgeschwader 'Richthofen'* experienced its true baptism of fire against the new enemy.

The one *Staffel* which had not accompanied III. *Gruppe* to Poix was Bruno Stolle's 8./JG 2. This was

At Brest-Guipavas 'Black 12' of 8. *Staffel* awaits the next scramble – the starter trolley is connected and the pilot's life-jacket and parachute pack are at the ready on the port tailplane

transferred instead back to Brest. The capital ships had long gone, but several *Flotillen* of U-boats were now based in ports along the French Atlantic coast. These boats had perforce to cross the Bay of Biscay at the start and end of each patrol, and to increase speed of passage they usually travelled on the surface. This in turn made them vulnerable to patrolling aircraft of RAF Coastal Command.

It thus became 8./JG 2's task to protect the U-boats against such attack. And although the enemy machines flying close to sea-level were not easy to detect and intercept, the *Staffel* claimed ten of their number – mostly twin-engined Bristol Beaufighters – in the space of as many weeks. But even as Stolle's pilots were accustoming themselves to operating at wave-top height, fresh danger suddenly threatened high overhead.

Having cut their teeth on the cross-Channel missions, the bombers of the Eighth Air Force now began to venture further afield. Their next targets were the huge concrete bunkers housing the Biscay-based U-boats. On 21 October a mixed force of B-17s and B-24 Liberators (see *Osprey Combat Aircraft 15 - B-24 Liberator units of the Eighth Air Force* for further

An Fw 190 warms up in preparation for take-off as contrails betray the enemy's presence high in the autumn sky

details) set out to attack Lorient. Heavy cloud prevented all but one group from finding the target. And it was this group, the 97th, which was presumably engaged by 8./JG 2. Three of their Fortresses failed to return, against the loss to the *Staffel* of Oberleutnant Otto Lütter.

Another three B-17s were reported missing after a similar raid against St Nazaire on 9 November, and nine days later a single Fortress went down during an attack on La Pallice, but two 8. *Staffel* Focke-Wulfs fell to the bombers' gunners. It was at this juncture that Stolle's embattled unit was reinforced by the arrival of the remainder of III. *Gruppe* at nearby Vannes-Meuçon.

Early in November the *Geschwader* had bid farewell to one of its most effervescent characters when 'Assi' Hahn took leave of III./JG 2 to assume command of II./JG 54 on the eastern front. Hahn, who had scored 68 victories – including four four-engined bombers – while with JG 2, would add a further 40 to his total before a deadstick landing behind enemy lines in February 1943 sentenced him to seven years of Soviet captivity.

It was thus under a new leader that III./JG 2 had departed Poix for the Atlantic coast. Egon Mayer was of a more analytical nature then his predecessor. He had studied the combat reports of all the actions against US heavy bombers to date, and was firmly of the opinion that the best chance of 'destroying or crippling the four-engined giants' was by frontal attack – the enemy pilots were at their most vulnerable, and the forward arc of defensive fire was at its weakest, from this direction. Mayer did not have long to wait to put his theories to the test.

On 23 November another mixed force of B-17s and B-24s was despatched against St Nazaire. Again, a solid layer of low-lying cloud hampered the bombers' attempts to find the target. Most aborted, but nine Fortresses reached their objective, only to be met during their bomb run by waves of Fw 190s attacking from dead ahead in *Ketten* of threes.

With Hauptmann Mayer leading, the Focke-Wulfs of III./JG 2 scythed through the bombers in the most successful single pass yet made by the Luftwaffe against the American 'heavies'. Four B-17s tumbled from the sky.

Although not yet perfected (Mayer's two wingmen sustained damage when they pulled up behind

Major Hans Hahn – in typical pose, and with the devoted 'Wumm' in attendance – relinquished command of III./JG 2 early in November 1942 to take over II./JG 54 in Russia

Hahn's successor was the erstwhile ***Staffelkapitän*** **of 7./JG 2, Oberleutnant Egon Mayer, who is seen here catching up with some paperwork beside the tail of his 'White 7'. The 48 victory bars on the rudder (unfortunately all but invisible in this photo) date it as mid-summer 1942 – by which time 'Chamberlain's hat' had finally given way to the 'cockerel's head'** ***Gruppe*** **badge . . .**

the bombers rather than diving away, and 7. *Staffel's* Unteroffizier Theodor Angele was brought down by return fire), the new tactic was seized upon by *General der Jagdflieger* Adolf Galland. After some refinement – instead of boring in straight and level, it was found that an approach from slightly above (the infamous 'twelve-o-clock high') gave the fighter a better chance of judging distances during the split-second closing speeds – the frontal attack became an accepted, and one of the most effective, methods of combating four-engined bombers. And none was more successful in carrying out such an assault than its originator, Egon Mayer.

On 30 December the Eighth Air Force was back over Lorient, and again it lost three B-17s (while claiming another 7./JG 2 Focke-Wulf). The year 1942 thus closed as had 1941, with the emphasis of the *Geschwader's* operations centred along the Atlantic seaboard. But there had been moves of late on the Channel front too.

On the last day of October 1942 the Fw 109s of 10.(*Jabo*)/JG 2 had combined with the fighter-bombers of JG 26 to mount a retaliatory 'tip-and-run' raid on Canterbury. All returned safely, but one of the escorting fighters, a machine of 5./JG 2, was hit by light anti-aircraft fire and crashed on the Kent coast.

The *Jabostaffel* would be less fortunate in the opening weeks of the new year. Five of its Focke-Wulfs were lost over the Channel – most, if not all, to RAF Typhoons (see *Osprey Aircraft of the Aces 27 - Typhoon/Tempest Aces of World War 2* for further details), despite the latter's reportedly 'disappointing' performance as an interceptor fighter – before Hauptmann Schümann's unit was redesignated 13./SKG 10 to become part of the new 'fast bomber' force in March 1943.

During that time another of JG 2's *Gruppen* had been enjoying a brief spell of almost total aerial superiority over terrain far removed from the wintry grey waters of the English Channel.

. . . which also adorns the cowling of this later Fw 190A-4. Although strikingly similar to, and often confused with, 'Assi' Hahn's own machine seen above, this is in fact one of Egon Mayer's early ***Gruppenkommandeur*** **aircraft. Differences to note (other than the rudder scoreboard) are the area of black paint above the wingroot to hide the exhaust stains, and the enlarged cowling intake (below the** ***Gruppe*** **badge) for the modified two-stage supercharger which was, at some point, fitted to this machine**

'Blue 6' of 10.(*Jabo*)/JG 2 is jacked up for weapons adjustment at Caen-Carpiquet in 1942

Operation *Torch* – the Anglo-American landings in north-west Africa on 8 November 1942 – had caused considerable consternation among the Wehrmacht High Command. Fearing that an invasion of southern France would shortly follow, German forces quickly occupied that area of France, including the Mediterranean coastline, which had hitherto been controlled by the Vichy French government. Among the units providing air cover was I./JG 2, which transferred from Dreux down to Marseilles-Marignane.

But after the expected enemy landing fleet failed to appear off the Riviera coast, the *Gruppe* returned to Normandy in mid-January 1943. It was then that the *Geschwader* lost another of its long-serving stalwarts as Hauptmann Erich Leie departed for Russia to take command of I./JG 51. Leie's victories with JG 2 had numbered 43 (including one four-engined bomber). Another 75 would be added while fighting on the eastern front, with Oberleutnant Leie finally being killed in the closing weeks of the war when *Kommodore* of JG 77.

Leie's place at the head of I./JG 2 was taken by 'Antek' Bolz, who had just relinquished command of II. *Gruppe* to Hauptmann Adolf Dickfeld. The latter was newly-arrived from the eastern front, where 115 kills with JG 52 had already earned him the Oak Leaves to his Knight's Cross.

Leaving Beaumont-le-Roger, II./JG 2 had also begun to stage southwards in the second week of November. Unlike I. *Gruppe*, however, its course took it not to an airfield in the south of France, but down the length of Italy to the island of Sicily – and thence across the Mediterranean to Tunisia. Here, it became part of the reinforcements which, it was hoped, would enable Axis forces to retain a foothold in North Africa.

On the ground any such hopes would be dashed by the combined might of the Allied 1st and 8th Armies. But for II./JG 2 the four-month sojourn in Tunisia would see its pilots recapture some of the success of the *Gruppe's* cross-Channel hey-day. Flying the only Fw 190 fighters in the

Oberleutnant Kurt Bühligen's 'White 1' was photographed shortly after its arrival at Kairouan, in Tunisia, in mid-December 1942. Note the array of tripod-mounted equipment on the hillock in the background, including a light AA machine-gun (left), a pair of periscope binoculars (centre) and what appears to be a sound locator (right)

North African theatre, the unit would claim some 150 enemy aircraft destroyed against just nine pilots killed in action.

But things did not get off to a good start, for two pilots were reported missing during the transfer flight and a third was killed in a B-17 bombing raid on Bizerta shortly after arrival. This raid, incidentally, was carried out by the 97th BG, which was the same group that had lost the three Fortresses to 8. *Staffel* over Lorient on 21 October, and which had since transferred from the Eighth to the Twelfth Air Force.

Based at Kairouan, II./JG 2's first Tunisian kill was a Spitfire credited to Oberleutnant Kurt Bühligen on 21 November. Bühligen proved the aptness of his nickname 'Bu-mann' ('Bogeyman') by quickly becoming the scourge of the Allied air forces. With 40 confirmed victories, he would emerge as the *Gruppe's* leading African *Experte*. Second came Leutnant Erich Rudorffer, *Staffelkapitän* of 6./JG 2, who was still in hospital in Paris recovering from severe wounds when the *Gruppe* had left for Tunisia.

Arriving in North Africa in mid-December, Rudorffer's logbook recorded his first contact with the enemy: '17 Bostons sighted in area of Cap Serrat'. These were American A-20s en route to bomb Mateur airfield, and Rudorffer's first kill was one of their RAF Spitfire escorts. On this same 18 December Bühligen claimed a pair of P-38s, and experienced NCO pilot Feldwebel Kurt Goltzsch got a third during another B-17 raid on Bizerta.

There were a spate of accidents at Kairouan during the second week of January, and in the first of these, on 8 January, Adolf Dickfeld was injured when his Fw 190 somersaulted on take-off after a wheel dug into a bomb crater. Erich Rudorffer was named as acting *Kommandeur*, an appointment which would be made official in May after the *Gruppe's* return to the Channel front.

II./JG 2's successes peaked in February. On the 3rd the *Gruppe* claimed a total of 12 victims, five falling to Bühligen (two P-39s, two P-40s and a Spitfire) and three to Goltzsch. Six days later they downed 16, with half of this number was credited to Rudorffer alone, including six P-40s in seven minutes! And on 15 February Rudorffer added another seven to his final Tunisian tally of 27.

This informal group shot includes II./JG 2's two leading scorers in Tunisia. The pilots are, from left to right, Olt Kurt Bühligen, Stabsarzt Krause (the *Gruppe's* medical officer), Olt Adolf Dickfeld and Lt Erich Rudorffer. The photo must have been taken at the turn of the year following Rudorffer's belated arrival in mid-December 1942, but before Dickfeld was wounded on 8 January 1943

On the debit side, Oberleutnant Wolf von Bülow, *Staffelkapitän* of 5./JG 2, lost his life when Kairouan was heavily bombed on 23 February. On 3 March – the day Kurt Bühligen brought down the first Spitfire Mk IX to be claimed by the Luftwaffe in Africa – 6. *Staffel's* Feldwebel Richard Ubelbacker was shot down in error over Ferryville by a *Rotte* of unidentified Bf 109s (although JGs 53 and 77 both submitted claims on this date, it is uncertain just who the guilty party was).

The final loss of the *Gruppe's* brief Tunisian venture was Unteroffizier Erich Engelbrecht of 4./JG 2, who fell victim to US-flown Spitfires west of Kairouan on 8 March. And the two B-17 Fortresses credited to Bühligen and Rudorffer four days later were among the last of the *Gruppe's* successes, for II./JG 2 was to be spared the closing two months of the war in North Africa, returning to Normandy in mid-March 1943.

The Bf 109Gs of Oberleutnant Julius Meimberg's 11./JG 2 had been despatched to Tunisia at the same time as the Focke-Wulfs of II. *Gruppe*. Unlike the latter, however, which had simply operated under temporary attachment to JG 53, Meimberg's high-altitude *Staffel* was officially incorporated into II./JG 53 and would not return to JG 2's control (see *Osprey Aircraft of the Aces 2 - Bf 109 Aces of the Mediterranean and North Africa* for further details).

Rudorffer's pilots were in for something of an unpleasant surprise when they got back to northern France. Tunisia may not have been the frying-pan, but the Channel front was fast assuming the proportions not just of a fire, but of a full-scale conflagration. As 1943 progressed, JG 2 would become increasingly enmeshed in an unwinnable war which was being waged against them on two fronts.

The *Gruppe's* Fw 190s may have enjoyed superiority in the air (except in terms of numbers!), but on the ground it was a different matter. These two desert tan machines, parked on II./JG 2's alternative landing strip at Tindja-South, have been heavily camouflaged against marauding Allied fighter-bombers

Not only were they expected to continue the tactical struggle against the traditional foe, the RAF – soon to be joined by the US Ninth Air Force – at medium and low-level, now they were also having to combat the growing numbers of high-altitude American heavy bombers overflying their airspace on their way to targets deep within occupied Europe, and even inside Germany itself. The *Geschwader* had become, in effect, the first line of defence in what was to develop into the Battle of the Reich.

Although proud of its status as a veteran frontline unit, JG 2's dual role was to cost it dear. By the end of 1943 almost 200 pilots would have been killed or posted missing. To put this in perspective, the *Geschwader's* losses for 1940, encompassing both the *Blitzkrieg* in the west and the Battle of Britain, totalled just 36! And although the bulk of 1943's casualty lists would be made up of newer, less experienced replacement pilots, they also contained a disturbing number of formation leaders, including nine *Staffelkapitäne*.

To help JG 2 fight its two-level war, further re-equipment now took place. Although the Fw 190 still retained a slight edge over the Spitfire IX, and was also regarded as a stable and efficient anti-bomber gun platform, its performance degraded sharply at altitude. It was therefore decided that I. and II./JG 2 should partially convert back on to the Bf 109.

Throughout the spring and early summer of 1943 the two *Gruppen* operated a mix of Fw 190As and Bf 109G-6s, the latter intended for higher-altitude missions, and to provide top cover for the Focke-Wulfs as and when necessary. But the mix of types within one unit did not prove altogether satisfactory, and I./JG 2 therefore reverted to the Fw 190 and II. *Gruppe* was re-equipped wholly with *Gustavs*, which it would retain until almost the very end of the war.

Against the background of growing casualty figures, JG 2's *alte Hasen* (literally 'old hares') continued to fight on. On 17 March Bruno Stolle's 29 victories won him the *Geschwader's* only Knight's Cross of 1943, and the following month Egon Mayer was awarded the Oak Leaves for taking his total to 63.

But, inevitably, it was the losses which dominated this chapter in JG 2's history as its opponents' strength grew. In addition to the fatalities, over 100 pilots were wounded during 1943. Nor was previous experience any

Wounded when his engine was hit in action against B-17s near Beaumont on 28 March 1943, Leutnant Georg-Peter Eder was lucky to escape with his life when his machine somersaulted upon landing at Beaumont. Here he is helped away by fellow 2. *Staffel* pilots

guarantee of safety, as two *Experten* recently arrived from the eastern front found to their cost.

Oberleutnant Georg-Peter Eder, formerly with JG 51, was lucky to survive twice being wounded during his stint of service with the *Jagdgeschwader 'Richthofen'* on the Channel front – the first occasion in action with 2. *Staffel* against B-17s near Beaumont-le-Roger on 18 March, and the second as *Staffelkapitän* of 5./JG 2 when he was forced to take to his parachute over Belgium on 5 November. Eder would, in fact, be wounded no fewer than 14 times between 1941 and 1945, ending the war with the Oak Leaves and flying Me 262 jets.

Eder's first *Staffelkapitän* in the west, Knight's Cross holder Leutnant Horst Hannig, who had been transferred in from JG 54 to assume command of 2./JG 2 at the beginning of 1943, was less fortunate. He met his

2./JG 2's *Staffelkapitän*, Leutnant Horst Hannig (foreground right, back to camera) was less fortunate than Eder, for he lost his life after clashing with RAF Spitfires on 15 May 1943. Note the elaborate 'eagle's head' motif on the Fw 190A-4 . . .

. . . which also decorates this 9. *Staffel* aircraft hidden in a tree-girt dispersal pen (note the rail for the tailwheel, allowing the fighter to be pushed even deeper under cover). It is photographs such as these which have led to speculation – as yet unproven – that I. and III. *Gruppen's* Focke-Wulfs could be distinguished by the former's 'eagle' having a rounded beak, as opposed to the latter's more angular contours. Another minor mystery – if that III. *Gruppe* vertical bar is yellow, what colour is the panel under the cowling?

end after clashing with a formation of some 40 Spitfires near Rocquancourt on 15 May. Although he managed to bail out, his parachute failed to open. Horst Hannig was awarded the Oak Leaves posthumously in January 1944.

May also saw the first of a number of command changes which took place in mid-1943 when Hauptmann Helmut Bolz relinquished the leadership of I. *Gruppe* to Hauptmann Erich Hohagen, who was another eastern front Knight's Cross winner and ex-member of JG 51.

Shortly thereafter Oberst Walter Oesau was notified of his imminent elevation to a staff position. But first he would celebrate his 30th birthday with the members of the *Geschwader* which he had commanded for almost exactly two years. The festivities were in full swing when, shortly after 1800 hrs on that 28 June, a formation of enemy bombers once again appeared over Beaumont-le-Roger.

This time, however, it was not half-a-dozen Lancasters fleetingly glimpsed at low-level, but 43 high-flying B-17s. Nor were they en route to another target elsewhere inside Germany. This time the objective was Beaumont itself. A carpet of bombs descended upon the one-time cornfield. The *Geschwaderstab* area and nearby buildings were particularly badly hit, and Oberfeldwebel Josef Höllerer of *Stab* I./JG 2 was killed, along with a further 19 ground personnel. Sixteen others were wounded.

Three days after the attack Oberst Oesau departed to become *Jafü Bretagne*. However, Walter Oesau would not remain behind a desk for long, for in October he assumed command of JG 1. With the earlier ban on combat flying conveniently forgotten, Oesau returned to operational flying, and his wartime total had reached 118 when he was finally shot down and killed during a dogfight with P-38 Lightnings over Germany's Eifel hills on 11 May 1944.

Hauptmann Egon Mayer, *Gruppenkommandeur* of III./JG 2, is seen in a lightweight summer jacket and wearing the Oak Leaves, awarded to him on 16 April 1943

Standing in one of Beaumont's typical blast pens, with starter trolley connected, the *Kommodore's* 'Green 13' is apparently not required today as Oberst Oesau strolls unconcernedly past

Despite similar reinforcement to the aircraft blast pens, JG 2's command HQ was badly damaged in the attack on Beaumont-le-Roger by 43 Fortresses of the Eighth Air Force on 28 June 1943. This earlier shot of the building, taken from the south, clearly shows the protective shoring (packed soil and timber) which also provided a walkway around the structure

Oesau's place at the head of the *Jagdgeschwader 'Richthofen'* was taken by Egon Mayer, and leadership of the Brittany-based III. *Gruppe* in turn passed to Hauptmann Bruno Stolle, long-time *Staffelkapitän* of 8./JG 2.

1943's last major change of command occurred in August when Erich Rudorffer was transferred to the eastern front to take over II./JG 54. The new *Kommandeur* of II./JG 2 was his erstwhile colleague in many a Tunisian dogfight, Kurt Bühligen.

By this time the *Geschwader* had suffered its first recorded losses against P-47 Thunderbolt escort fighters of the Eighth Air Force (see *Osprey Aircraft of the Aces 24 - P-47 Thunderbolt Aces of the Eighth Air Force* for further details). Their appearance had tightened the pressure another notch, and on 15 August it was II. *Gruppe's* turn to experience at first hand the growing muscle of the 'Mighty Eighth' when its Vitry-en-Artois base was specifically targeted by over 80 B-17s. As well as the three pilots shot down

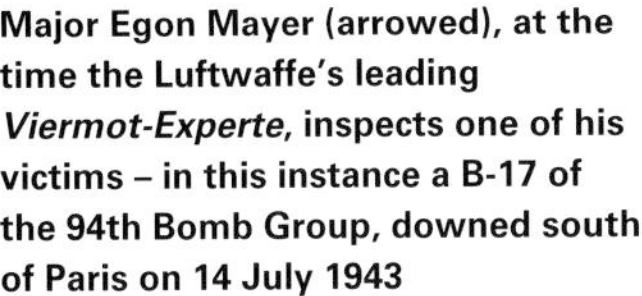

Major Egon Mayer (arrowed), at the time the Luftwaffe's leading *Viermot-Experte*, inspects one of his victims – in this instance a B-17 of the 94th Bomb Group, downed south of Paris on 14 July 1943

Another aircraft to meet its end in a cornfield – already harvested and near Aachen, in Germany – was this broken-backed *Gustav* of II. *Gruppe*. Leutnant Paul Müngersdorff (standing behind fuselage cross) surveys the wreckage of his 'Black 7' on 12 August 1943

Gruppenkommandeur Kurt Bühligen pins the German Cross in Gold to the tunic of Oberleutnant Kurt Goltzsch. This award was just one rank below the Knight's Cross, which Goltzsch would later receive in his hospital bed after being mortally wounded crash-landing his battle-damaged fighter

by the bombers' escort, ground casualties included five killed and eight wounded.

Worse was to follow 24 hours later when the Eighth Air Force struck at Le Bourget and Poix airfields. JG 2 suffered its highest single day's casualties of the entire year, losing nine pilots killed and six wounded – two of the latter forced-landing on the very airfields under attack. Among the fatalities was Oberleutnant Ferdinand Müller, *Staffelkapitän* of 1./JG 2. Two further *Staffelkapitäne* would be lost in action against the Eighth's 'heavies' before August was out, and a third was mortally wounded crash-landing following a duel with Spitfires near Monschy on 4 September.

The latter pilot was 5./JG 2's Oberleutnant Kurt Goltzsch, whose long career with the *Geschwader* had begun as an NCO pilot. Since then he had scored 43 kills, 14 of them in Tunisia. After more than a year in hospital, during which time he was awarded the Knight's Cross, Goltzsch finally succumbed to the spinal injuries he had sustained in the crash.

On 6 September the boot was, briefly, on the other foot. That date's scheduled mission to Stuttgart would prove to be 'one of the most costly fiascos in Eighth Air Force history'. Scattered by heavy cloud, B-17s came down all over western Europe, from Switzerland to the south coast of England. Three of the 45 Fortresses lost were claimed by *Kommodore* Egon Mayer in the space of just 19 minutes.

But such successes were becoming ever rarer. On 16 September the *Kommandeur* of I./JG 2, Hauptmann Erich Hohagen, crash-landed wounded after attacking 16 B-17s south of Rennes. And among the 12 casualties suffered exactly one week later, on 23 September, was 'Sepp' Wurmheller, *Staffelkapitän* of 9./JG 2, who was wounded by bomb splinters while attempting an emergency landing at Vannes-Meuçon.

It was at this juncture that JG 2, like many other *Jagdgeschwader*, was reorganised on a four-*Staffel*-per-*Gruppe* basis. This was intended to increase each individual *Geschwader's* combat strength. In the case of JG 2, however, three additional *Staffeln* – 10., 11. and 12. – had already been activated some time earlier. Just how these three were now incorporated into the new framework of the *Geschwader* is perhaps best illustrated by the following table;

Oberleutnant Josef Wurmheller, *Staffelkapitän* of 9./JG 2, was photographed in September 1943 when his score stood at 81. The 'double' American kill bars on the rudder indicate US heavy bombers (which earned a pilot three 'points' – as opposed to a fighter's one – in the Luftwaffe's complicated awards system)

I. *Gruppe*: 1. *Staffel* - as before
2. *Staffel* - as before
3. *Staffel* - as before
4. *Staffel* - ex-11. *Staffel*

II. *Gruppe*: 5. *Staffel* - as before
6. *Staffel* - as before
7. *Staffel* - ex-4. *Staffel*
8. *Staffel* - ex-12. *Staffel*

III. *Gruppe*: 9. *Staffel* - as before
10. *Staffel* - new
11. *Staffel* - ex-7. *Staffel*
12. *Staffel* - ex-8. *Staffel*

Pilots and groundcrew of 4./JG 2 relax in front of a Bf 109G-6 *'Kanonenboot'* ('gunboat' – note the underwing 20 mm cannon gondola) at Evreux in the autumn of 1943, shortly before the *Staffel* was renumbered 7./JG 2 in line with the *Geschwader's* restructuring

RETREAT AND DEFEAT

The restructuring of late 1943, which had been intended to boost the *Geschwader's* strength and combat capability, proved in the event to be of very little practical help. And what limited immediate benefit there may have been was nullified at the turn of the year by the appearance of the P-51B Mustang. This outstanding long-range US escort fighter – a marriage of British engine to American airframe – was able to accompany the Eighth Air Force's heavy bombers into the furthest most reaches of Hitler's Reich (see *Osprey Aircraft of the Aces 1 - P-51 Mustang Aces of the Eighth Air Force* for further details).

Together with the newer marks of Griffon-powered Spitfires then entering RAF squadron service (see *Osprey Aircraft of the Aces 5 - Late Mark Spitfire Aces 1942-45* for further details), the American fighter dashed all hopes of the *Jagdwaffe* being able to regain the upper hand in western Europe.

Faced by opponents who now enjoyed undisputed superiority not only in terms of numbers but also in quality, it is little wonder that JG 2's grim casualty figures of 1943 should continue unabated into 1944. In fact, as spring approached and Allied air forces began softening-up Normandy – the very heart of the *Geschwader's* defence area – its losses became ever more grievous.

The *'Richthofen'* pilots were still fighting back to the best of their ability, however. In January 1944 the *Geschwader* was credited with its 2000th kill, but the rate of attrition was unremitting. That same month's 19 combat fatalities included three more *Staffelkapitäne* and the *Geschwader-Adjutant*. Hauptmann Fritz Edelmann, who had served in that office since taking over from Erich Leie back in May 1942, was killed in action north of Paris on 30 January.

Representative of the pilots bearing the brunt of the Allied onslaught in the run-up to D-Day is this trio from 8./JG 2 pictured at Creil in the winter of 1943-44. They are, from left to right, Uffz Gerhard Querengässer, Lt Kabbe (*Staffelkapitän*) and Lt Wolfgang Harnisch. Querengässer, who had flown as wingman to Oesau, was injured twice in 1944 (on 23 March and 26 June), as was Harnisch (both times against P-47s, on 24 February and 27 March). The latter pilot finally succumbed in a third clash with a pair of Thunderbolts near Le Mans on 20 June 1944

Recovered from wounds sustained on 29 January (also in combat against P-47s, near Bastogne), Oberleutnant Gerd Schaedle, *Staffelkapitän* of 5./JG 2, prepares to take off from Creil in the spring of 1944. Here, the underwing cannon armament of the Bf 109G-6 is very apparent

Although the pressure from across the Channel was constant, the situation on other fronts was, if anything, even more precarious.

The Allied advance in Italy, albeit slow, was gradually opening up airbases which threatened the whole of southern Europe. Late in January 1944 Hauptmann Erich Hohagen's I. *Gruppe* was transferred to Aix-en-Provence in the south of France, its arrival coinciding with heavy raids by the Fifteenth Air Force on Luftwaffe bomber bases in the area. On 27 January 2. *Staffel* lost two pilots, one against B-17s over Aix and the other to Spitfires north of Toulon.

The object of the Fifteenth Air Force raids had been to disrupt German bombing attacks on shipping off the Anzio beachheads. These Anglo-American landings to the south of Rome were an attempt to break the Italian deadlock, and attracted fierce Luftwaffe resistance. Elements of I./JG 2 were moved from Aix to central Italy, where they deployed on airstrips at Canino, Castiglione and Diabolo. The *Gruppe's* Fw 190s and Bf 109Gs (4. *Staffel* – the ex-11./JG 2 – was still equipped with the *Gustav*) were soon thrown into the action, being committed over the Anzio-Nettuno beachheads and beyond.

One of the most successful pilots during the *Gruppe's* ten-week involvement in the Italian campaign was officer-candidate Oberfeldwebel Siegfried Lemke, *Staffelführer* of 1./JG 2. But in Italy, too, individual successes were being far outweighed by a scale of casualties which was the inevitable consequence of the enemy's overwhelming local air superiority. And such losses were not all sustained above the immediate area of the beachheads. On 3 March over 80 heavily-escorted Fifteenth Air Force B-24s were despatched against Viterbo airfield and the landing ground at Canino. A group of supporting P-47s claimed seven Luftwaffe fighters, among them two Fw 190s and a Bf 109 of I./JG 2. Another 4. *Staffel Gustav* fell victim to the Allies' weight of numbers when Unteroffizier Erich Gross was shot down in a dogfight with 20 to 25 Spitfires over the historic abbey of Cassino on 17 March.

One of I./JG 2's last engagements in Italy occurred on 6 April when the eight remaining Bf 109s of 4. *Staffel* were returning to Aix-en-Provence. Nearing the coast, the *Gustavs* were attacked over Grosseto by some two-dozen Allied fighters. In the fierce dogfight which followed, one of the enemy – described as an RAF Mustang (probably from No 260 Sqn) – was claimed shot down. But two of the Bf 109s were badly hit, one pilot bailng out and the other surviving a forced landing. The remaining six made it safely back to Aix. After a further month of 'relative peace and quiet' in southern France, I./JG 2 flew back to their base at Creil, north of Paris, in early May.

The situation on the Channel front – bad enough at the beginning of the year – had worsened dramatically since. While I. *Gruppe* had been on detachment in the south, the *Jagdgeschwader 'Richthofen'* had lost two *Kommodores*.

Leutnant Wolfgang Fischer (right) of I. *Gruppe* was twice on the receiving end of Allied fighter attacks during 1944. He was forced to crash-land his Bf 109G after tangling with a superior number of RAF Mustangs over Grosseto on 6 April. After returning to his unit by road (taking time off for a little sight-seeing in Genoa, where this 'holiday snap' was taken, on the way), Fischer would be shot down by shipboard anti-aircraft gunners on D-Day+1

A grim-faced Oberstleutnant Egon Mayer reportedly pictured early in 1944. Unfortunately, no photographs of Mayer's 'blue-nosed' Fw 190A-6 appear to have survived . . .

The first to fall had been Egon Mayer. On 2 March Mayer was leading his *Stabsschwarm* at the head of III. *Gruppe* – some 14 Fw 190s in all – when he sighted and attacked a formation of B-17s in the vicinity of Sedan (scene of the famous 'Day of the Fighters' of nearly four years earlier). But, intent on his diving pass through the bombers, Egon Mayer had failed to spot a separate group of 29 P-47s some 5000 ft (1500 m) above.

The Thunderbolts found themselves perfectly positioned for a classic 'bounce'. They in turn dived upon the Fw 190s, two of which went down immediately. Four others were shot down in the ensuing dogfight, which reportedly 'covered more than 40 miles (65 km) of sky before it was over'.

Although not absolutely certain, Mayer's machine was probably the one described by its opponent as having 'a blue nose and belly, and not the yellow nose that the other enemy planes had'. Taking hits at 400 yards (365 m) range in the nose and cockpit area, this aircraft was seen to make a violent snap roll, turn over on to its back, and enter the overcast in a vertical dive, with no indication of recovery. Mayer's Focke-Wulf crashed to earth 1.5 miles (2.5 km) south of Montmédy.

At the time of his loss Oberstleutnant Egon Mayer was the Luftwaffe's leading *Viermot-Experte*, with 25 four-engined bombers to his credit. It was a cruel twist of fate that the man who, only a month earlier on 5 February 1944, had become the first to achieve 100 victories on the western front, should then himself fall victim so shortly afterwards to an almost completely untried and 'greenhorn' unit. The P-47s of the Ninth Air Force's 365th Fighter Group had been declared operational just ten days before (see *Osprey Aircraft of the Aces 30 - P-47 Thunderbolt Aces of the Ninth and Fifteenth Air Forces* for further details).

The announcement of the award of the Swords to Egon Mayer's Oak Leaves was made on the day of his death. His replacement as *Kommodore* of JG 2 was to be Major Kurt Ubben, who had been *Gruppenkommandeur* of III./JG 77 for the last two-and-a-half years. Ubben took leave of his *Gruppe* in Rumania (where it was guarding the airfields of Ploesti) on 10 March. He was already wearing the Oak Leaves, and had amassed 110 aerial victories to date.

But the western front in the spring of 1944 was no respecter of reputations, however illustrious. Without adding to his score, Major Ubben was lost in similar circumstances to Mayer, caught by a group of P-47s west of Reims on 27 April. Although he managed to get out of his heavily-armed Fw 190A-8/R2, Ubben's parachute failed to open (some sources giving insufficient altitude as the cause, others citing an improperly fastened harness).

Kurt Ubben was the fourth JG 2 *Kommodore* to be killed in action – the highest number lost by any *Jagdgeschwader* during the course of the war. The authorities did not look so far afield for the officer who was to take his place. Kurt Bühligen had joined the Luftwaffe in 1936 as a chief mechanic. His entire flying career since 1940 had been with JG 2.

Having been awarded the Oak Leaves on 2 March for 96 kills, Major Bühligen passed command of his II. *Gruppe* to Hauptmann Georg Schröder and, at the beginning of May 1944, became the tenth, and final, *Kommodore* of the *Jagdgeschwader 'Richthofen'*.

The loss of the two *Kommodores* in quick succession may have dominated the spring of 1944, but it was the constant haemorrhaging among

. . . unlike this shot of his successor Kurt Bühligen's Fw 190, which boasted an unusual splinter camouflage finish and a unique set of *Kommodore* chevrons and bars

the rank-and-file, and of formation leaders at the lower levels, which was the real drain on the *Geschwader's* strength. February's losses had totalled 26 killed or missing, plus 15 wounded. Among the latter was ex-JG 51 Knight's Cross holder Hauptmann Herbert Huppertz. But Huppertz's injuries were not severe, and in March he was given command of III. *Gruppe* when Hauptmann Stolle was posted to the Luftwaffe's gunnery school – Bruno Stolle would later return to operational flying as *Kommandeur* of I./JG 11.

Three *Staffelkapitane* were lost in March, and a fourth in April. All but one had fallen to P-47s. Despite the P-51's predominance in much post-war aviation literature, many JG 2 pilots, unlike their comrades flying purely high-altitude Defence of the Reich operations, confess to finding the portly, eight-and-a-half-ton Thunderbolt by far the tougher adversary.

The pre-invasion period reached a climax on 30 April. On that day alone the *Geschwader* suffered 13 casualties in a series of engagements with US fighters – both P-47s and P-51s. May's losses included two more *Staffelkapitäne*, one, flying an Fw 190, being downed by a trio of US P-47s near Châteaudun, the other's *Gustav* falling victim to six RAF Typhoons north of Paris.

Then, late in May, even as Allied invasion troops were converging on the embarkation ports along England's southern coast, JG 2 – almost incredible as it may seem in hindsight – began pulling out of the Channel front area it had defended for so long!

Either the *Geschwader* was hurting too much from the relentless 'softening-up' of the previous weeks (serviceability figures for 25 May show it to be at less than a third of full strength), or the Allies' elaborate subterfuges as to the precise date and place of the invasion was forcing its wider dispersal.

On 4 April 1944 Major Kurt Bühligen (left) received his Oak Leaves from the Führer. Similarly honoured were the next in line, nightfighter *Experte* Major Hans-Joachim Jabs, and bomber commanders Majors Berhard Jope (KG 100) and Hansgeorg Bätcher (I./KG 4) beyond

A JG 2 ordnance NCO (note the crossed rifles on his lower left sleeve) leans nonchalantly against a heavily-armed Fw 190A-6. It was with underwing rockets such as these that I. *Gruppe* attacked shipping off 'Gold' on D-Day

Whatever the reason, Hauptmann Huppertz's III. *Gruppe* was ordered to vacate Cormeilles for Fontenay le Comte, north of La Rochelle, on the Atlantic coast. II./JG 2's departure from Creil on 28 May is easier to explain. Leaving their worn-out *Gustavs* behind, Georg Schröder and his pilots were returning to Germany by road and rail to re-equip with newer sub-variants of the Bf 109G-6. Lastly, on 3 June – less than 72 hours before those self-same invasion troops stormed ashore on Normandy's beaches – the four *Staffeln* of I./JG 2 were withdrawn from the landing grounds around Cormeilles, to which they had been redeployed several weeks earlier, and retired to similar strips in the region of Nancy some 200 miles (320 km) to the east.

Despite their distance from the landing beaches, I. and III./JG 2 were quick to respond to news of the invasion. Leutnant Wolfgang Fischer, who had flown *Gustavs* with 4. *Staffel* in Italy (it was he who had been forced to land after being attacked by RAF Mustangs on 6 April), but had since converted to the Fw 190, remembers D-Day vividly. His experiences may not have been typical, but they are certainly enlightening;

'At about 0500 hrs on the morning of 6 June a motorcyclist pulled up outside my quarters, yelled my name and the one word – "Invasion!" He drove me out to the strip and we quickly took off back to Creil.

'There we waited around for two hours while our aircraft were fitted with underwing rockets. We had been briefed to attack the landing fleet, and I spent the time trying to work out how to hit a ship with these things. Their aiming instructions were brief and to the point. "At 1000 metres (3300 ft) range aim off 80 metres (260 ft) to the left". I decided a beam attack would offer the best chance of success.

'At 0930 hrs 12 of us took off for Vers-sur-mer (a village along the British 'Gold' landing beach). Hohagen was not flying this mission – we were being led instead by Hauptmann Wurmheller. The sky was seven-tenths covered in thick cumulus. We kept spotting swarms of Allied fighters in the clear patches but successfully avoided them all, wanting first to fire our rockets at the shipping.

'At about 1000 hrs we flew over Bayeux. Parts of the town were already burning. We continued on out over the Bay of the Seine for a short distance, hoping to achieve surprise by attacking from the seaward side. From our altitude of some 3000 metres (9850 ft) I could see the entire coastline from the mouth of the Orne in the east to St Maire-Eglise in the west. Offshore lay a huge armada – battleships on the outermost edges, transports nearer to land, and tiny landing craft heading in to the beaches.

'Dodging between the fat, dark shapes of the barrage balloons, I was the only one lucky enough to find a fair-sized vessel – it could have been a Liberty ship – almost directly in my path. It was turning slightly to port, so I aimed off a full ship's length ahead and pressed the red button normally used to jettison the ventral fuel tank.

'For a split-second I seemed to be enveloped in flames. Relieved of the weight of the rockets the machine leaped upwards. Recovering from the shock, I watched the twin points of light head down towards the target. One exploded on the stern of the ship. The other disappeared in a fountain of water just behind her.

'I released the two launch tubes and quickly built up speed in a shallow dive towards the shore and home. I fired at the beaches as I passed overhead, but it wasn't safe to linger because of the numerous enemy fighter patrols.'

Wolfgang Fischer landed safely at 1045 hrs – not at Creil, but on a racecourse in the grounds of a small chateau at nearby Senlis. It was part of the Luftwaffe's contingency plans in the event of invasion to disperse its fighters on small, hard-to-find landing strips such as this.

At Senlis Fischer experienced what he later described as a 'grotesque' situation. While Major Hohagen and his *Stabsschwarm* flew a single mission, which netted the *Gruppenkommandeur* a Typhoon, the rest of the unit was given the afternoon off! Fischer and his fellow pilots took the opportunity to enjoy the amenities of the local swimming pool – basking in the summer sun with the local populace while a solitary P-51 circled aimlessly some 2000 metres (6500 ft) overhead. But all good things must come to an end;

'It wasn't until the evening that things started to happen again. At about 1930 hrs Hauptmann Huppertz, the *Kommandeur* of III. *Gruppe*, landed on our strip with five of his Focke-Wulfs. When they took off again some thirty minutes later, I and two of my comrades accompanied them. We were flying almost due west at about 400 metres (1300 ft), heading for the scene of the airborne landings around Caen, when we sighted a dozen P-51s circling and strafing one of our road convoys.

'All thoughts of the Caen mission were abandoned. We had to help our troops on the ground below. The Mustangs were so engrossed in their work that they failed to notice us. Jettisoning our long-range tanks, we eight Fw 190s climbed to 1200 metres (3900 ft) to reach the ideal height and position from which to launch our attack.

'Before diving on them from behind, each of us had had ample opportunity to select, quite literally, "his" Mustang. "Mine" had just completed a pass on some vehicles crossing a bridge, and was on the point of pulling up, when I got on his tail – still undetected – and caught him fair and square. The Mustang slid into a gentle dive and smashed into the river bank at the foot of a large tree, which immediately burst into flames from ground to tip like a huge candle.

'We landed back at Senlis at around 2130 hrs – it was already getting quite dark – to great excitement. A recording truck was waiting and we were interviewed live on the radio. At that time eight victories without loss was regarded as something quite exceptional.'

In fact, D-Day itself was the *Geschwader's* most successful day of the entire Normandy campaign. Between them, I. and III./JG 2 had accounted for no fewer than 18 Allied fighters. The first, just before midday, had been a P-47 claimed by Major Kurt Bühligen. It was the *Geschwaderkommodore's* 99th victory. The highest scorer was Herbert Huppertz, who had already downed three Typhoons before being credited with two of the eight P-51s despatched near Evreux.

On the debit side, each *Gruppe* had lost just one Focke-Wulf. A 3. *Staffel* machine had crashed en route from Nancy back to Creil, and one unfortunate pilot of 11./JG 2, newly flown in from the Atlantic seaboard, was promptly shot down by 'friendly' flak south of Rouen.

Two further losses were recorded on D+1. The first was another III./JG 2 pilot, this time of 10. *Staffel*, who also ventured too close to Rouen's trigger-happy flak defences. The second was Wolfgang Fischer.

Again armed with underwing rockets, Leutnant Fischer was this time flying wingman to Major Hohagen at the head of 20 Fw 190s briefed to attack both the shipping off 'Gold' and the Würzburg radar station atop the Pointe du Hoc, which had been captured by the enemy. Having missed with his rockets, Fischer dived to rake a large LST with cannon fire. Caught by the ship's anti-aircraft gunners – 'it was like flying through a glowing spider's web', he recalls – Fischer was wounded and forced to bail out of his badly damaged fighter. The wind carried him back to shore, where he was extricated from a minefield by a pair of British soldiers.

On that same 7 June JG 2 claimed ten Allied fighters over the beachhead area. Three fell to 1. *Staffel's* newly-commissioned Leutnant Siegfried Lemke, whilst 'Sepp' Wurmheller's early-morning Typhoon north of Caen had taken his score to 98. But it was the brace of P-47s

A post-mission drink back at Creil on the evening of D-Day marked *Kommodore* Bühligen's century of kills – he can be seen in the centre wearing a life jacket. The bareheaded figure on his right is Oberstleutnant Josef 'Pips' Priller, CO of neighbouring JG 26, who had just scored his 98th victory. Note that the aircraft on this occasion is not Bühligen's splinter-camouflaged Fw 190

'We congratulate you on the 100th' – the placard says it all. Bühligen still hasn't had time to remove his life jacket

claimed by Bühligen in the evening, also over Caen, which led to the biggest celebrations back at Creil – the first of the two US fighters had given the *Geschwaderkommodore* his century.

The jubilation was to be short-lived, for after 48 hours of success, the *Geschwader's* fortunes again began to decline as the sheer weight of Allied air superiority extracted a fearsome toll. As before, it was the sketchily-trained replacements who were bearing the brunt, many not even surviving their first operational sortie. But experienced formation leaders were also being lost. Among the nearly 70 casualties sustained in the last three weeks of June were eight *Staffelkapitäne* and three *Gruppenkommandeure*.

Although 8 June's kills and casualties were numerically equal at three each (among the former were a P-51 apiece for Wurmheller and Lemke), one of the trio of losses was Hauptmann Huppertz, shot down by P-47s near Caen. Huppertz (who would be awarded the Oak Leaves posthumously on 24 June) was immediately replaced at the head of III. *Gruppe* by Josef Wurmheller. But the seemingly indestructible 'Sepp's' days were numbered too.

After emulating the *Kommodore's* feat by downing a pair of P-47s near Caen (on 12 June) to bring his score to 101, Hauptmann Josef Wurmheller would add just one more Allied fighter to his total before he was himself killed in a dogfight with Canadian Spitfires north of Alençon on 22 June.

III./JG 2's third *Kommandeur* in the space of a fortnight was Siegfried Lemke, ex-*Staffelkapitän* of 1./JG 2, and newly decorated with the Knight's Cross for 47 confirmed kills.

By this time Hauptmann Schröder's II. *Gruppe* had returned to the Normandy front. The first Bf 109Gs flew in from Cologne to a small field near Baron, south-east of Creil, on 14 June. Three days later they undertook their first operation, and promptly lost six of their *Gustavs*, two colliding on take-off, and the others shot down by P-47s and anti-aircraft fire.

Three days later still (with another Bf 109 having been written off in the interim when it somersaulted upon landing), II./JG 2 lost five more machines, again including two in take-off accidents. The small, disguised landing strips, each of which was allocated its own code-name – Baron, for example, rejoicing in '*Sauwechsel*' (literally 'Boar's haunt') – may have offered their occupants some degree of safety from roving Allied fighter-bombers, but they were not the easiest places from which to operate, especially for inadequately trained youngsters straight out of flying school.

All smiles as the *Kommodore* presents Leutnant Siegfried Lemke with his Knight's Cross, awarded on 14 June for 47 confirmed victories. Lemke would lead III. *Gruppe* for the last ten months of the war

But it was, of course, in the air that the *Geschwader* was suffering most. As June turned to July they were losing up to a dozen pilots a day. The campaign assumed a savage new complexion on 25 June, for one of that day's twelve casualties was found in his parachute, his body riddled with machine-gun bullets. But whether the unfortunate pilot was deliberately targeted, or had been caught in the cross-fire of the fierce dogfight between II. *Gruppe's Gustavs* and US P-38s and P-51s west of Bernay, remains open to interpretation.

Although II./JG 2 could still field 17 serviceable Bf 109s out of the 50+ they had brought back from Germany 12 days earlier, I. and III. *Gruppen* had by now been fought almost to extinction, possessing just five and eight serviceable Focke-Wulfs respectively.

On 11 July Erich Hohagen handed his last few Fw 190s over to Siegfried Lemke's III./JG 2, and entrained with his surviving pilots for Husum, in Schleswig-Holstein, for re-equipment and reinforcement. For the next month the Messerschmitts and Focke-Wulfs of II. and III./JG 2 carried on the fight. Despite their own paucity of numbers – it was a rare day when either *Gruppe's* serviceability returns reached double figures – they managed to claim some 16 kills between them. But they lost nearly three times that number of pilots during the same period.

One such, shot down near Argentan on 15 July, would have been just another entry on the lengthening list of casualties were it not for his illustrious name. 10. *Staffel's* Oberfähnrich Ruthard von Richthofen was a distant relative of the famous 'Red Baron' himself. He was one of at least two young members of the von Richthofen family to be killed in action with the Luftwaffe in World War 2 (the other being an Fw 190 ground-attack pilot on the eastern front, who was posted missing just a month before).

On 13 August Hauptmann Hohagen led I. *Gruppe* back into the fray, but by now the Battle of Normandy was effectively lost, and the *Jagdwaffe* – outnumbered in the air and hunted on the ground – was a spent force. Fresh blood simply gave rise to fresh losses. In the last two weeks of the campaign the rebuilt I./JG 2 would suffer a further 20 casualties.

Six pilots were lost on their first day back in action alone, although the *Gruppe* did manage to claim four of their opponents – a trio of P-47s and a single P-38 – during the bitter dogfight south-east of Chartres. It was on this same 14 August that *Geschwaderkommodore* Kurt Bühligen was awarded the Swords to his Oak Leaves for 104 victories.

The end could not be postponed much longer. Nine days later the last seven surviving pilots of Siegfried Lemke's III. *Gruppe* returned to Germany to refit and make up their numbers. And on 25 August the remainder of JG 2 began to pull out of France.

During the same period Hauptmann Walter Matoni would see service as *Kommandeur* of both I. and II. *Gruppen* (from September-December 1944 and January-February 1945 respectively)

A formal portrait of Oberstleutnant Kurt Bühligen, tenth and final *Kommodore* of the *Jagdgeschwader 'Richthofen'*, wearing the Swords to his Oak Leaves

Their destination was a group of airfields north of Frankfurt, not far from their original jumping-off points for the *Blitzkrieg* in the West. The *Geschwader* had come full circle. And here they would stay until the final chaotic weeks of the war.

While II. *Gruppe's* dozen *Gustavs* first staged via Eschborn for reinforcement, before taking up residence at Nidda, the Fw 190s of I./JG 2 had arrived at Merzhausen by the first week of September. But the withdrawal to the Homeland won them little respite, for on 9 September they lost eight Focke-Wulfs, mainly to P-47s, to the north and east of their new base. And three days later another eight Fw 190s fell victim to a group of 50+ Mustangs in the Wiesbaden area. This set the pattern for the immediate future as the *Gruppe* continued to struggle against mounting odds.

On 28 September *Luftflotte 3* was redesignated *Luftwaffenkommando-West*. JG 2 (and JG 26) remained subordinated to the new command, still jealously protective of their position on the Luftwaffe's Order of Battle as the west's two 'frontline' *Jagdgeschwader*. But based now on German soil, they were becoming inextricably linked with those Homeland defence units operating under the direct control of *Luftflotte Reich*.

The two *Geschwader* would even be allotted official Defence of the Reich rear fuselage bands, but there are members of JG 2 who are still adamant that no *'Richthofen'* machine ever sported the colourful yellow-white-yellow markings assigned to them.

On the day that *Lfl. 3* was transformed into *Lw.Kdo. West*, Hauptmann Erich Hohagen, who had suffered severe head injuries in a forced landing, passed command of I. *Gruppe* to Hauptmann Walter Matoni, ex-*Staffelkapitän* of 5./JG 26.

In mid-October, having completed re-equipment at Königsberg in der Neumark, to the north-east of Berlin, III./JG 2 arrived at Altenstadt with its new Bf 109s. With II. *Gruppe* already sharing Nidda with the *Geschwaderstab*, JG 2 was once more fully deployed at the front.

Although still sustaining losses, casualties had now become far fewer than during the blood-letting of the recent Normandy campaign. During November the *Geschwader* even managed to increase its numbers slightly (from 78 serviceable machines at the beginning of the month to 91 by its close). This was partly due to the fact that fewer missions were being flown as stocks of aviation fuel began to run dangerously low. But it was also the result of a deliberate policy on the part of *General der Jagdflieger* Adolf Galland.

Galland was conserving his day-fighters' strength in preparation for one massive and decisive assault on the US heavy bombers now parading at will – and in their thousands – across the face of the Reich. When the time was right, *der grofle Schlag* (the 'Big Blow') would knock hundreds of those bombers out of the sky, and, he reasoned, weaken the Eighth Air Force's will to mount further attacks.

As well as building up its numbers, the *Jagdwaffe* was also receiving new equipment. For JG 2 this meant the addition of Bf 109Ks to II. *Gruppe's* late-model *Gustavs*, and the start of III./JG 2's conversion on to the 'long-nose' Fw 190D-9.

But equipment of a less welcome nature was delivered to JG 2's bases in December – bomb racks. Galland's 'Big Blow' had been postponed, and his carefully husbanded fighters 'hijacked' to take part in an even more ambitious undertaking: the Führer's planned counter-offensive in the Ardennes.

In almost an exact re-run of the tactics which had won the Battle of France over four years earlier, 21 German divisions were to launch a surprise attack out of the wooded hills sitting astride the German-Belgian border. This time the objective was to be Antwerp, but the strategic aim was the same as before – to split the Allied ground forces in two.

Operation *'Wacht am Rhein'* ('Watch on the Rhine', a misleadingly defensive code-name, and now more commonly known as the 'Battle of the Bulge') began on 16 December. The launch date had been purposely chosen to coincide with a forecast spell of bad weather which, it was hoped, would nail the enemy's superior air power firmly to the ground.

The cloudy conditions may have hampered intervention by the UK-based 'heavies', but they had less effect on the Allies' tactical air forces already on the continent. On 17 December a formation of rocket-armed Fw 190s of III./JG 2, escorted by some two dozen II. *Gruppe* Messerschmitts, was ordered to attack US artillery positions west of Monschau. Engaged by P-47s, four of the *Gustavs* were shot down. I./JG 2 lost an equal number of Focke-Wulfs in a separate action against P-47s that same day.

18 December's three casualties, which all fell to P-47s on the northern flank of the 'Bulge', included two of II./JG 2's new Bf 109K-4s. But it was the slight improvement in the weather five days later which brought out the Ninth Air Force's medium bombers, and which led to JG 2's heaviest single day's losses of the brief 'campaign'. Together with elements of JGs 3 and 11, the *Geschwader* engaged some 60 B-26 Marauders attacking rail targets on the west bank of the Rhine.

Although 16 of the bombers were brought down, their escorting fighters made the assailants pay a high price. Half of JG 2's ten casualties came from III. *Gruppe*, and among the five was a 12. *Staffel* Fw 190D-9 – one of the first 'long-noses' lost by the *Geschwader*.

On 24 December a high-pressure area finally brought clear skies over western Europe, and unleashed the Eighth's 'heavies'. Everything that could fly was ordered into the air to help the embattled ground troops. High on the list of targets were the Luftwaffe's airfields, with over 400 Fortresses targeting JG 2's bases north of Frankfurt alone. Most of the *Geschwader* was absent, operating over the Bastogne area of the battlefield, but two pilots who valiantly tried to defend their airfields were shot down by the bombers' P-51 escort fighters, one over Nidda, the other above Merzhausen.

The *Geschwader* lost at least three more aircraft in the final weeks of 1944 – a pair of *Gustavs* north-west of Bonn on 27 December and a solitary 'long-nose' of I. *Gruppe* over Koblenz four days later.

Just what the Fw 190D-9 was doing some 40 miles (65 km) from base is unclear, for most of the *Jagdgruppen* in the west were grounded on that New Year's Eve being readied for the major operation scheduled for first light the following morning. Now that it was too late – German troops were already retreating from the 'Bulge' – Adolf Galland had finally been given the go-ahead for his *'große Schlag'*.

It had been decreed from on high, however, that the 'Big Blow' was not to be aimed at the Eighth Air Force in the air, but against airfields in the

Low Countries and France, occupied by units of the enemy's tactical air forces.

Each of the 11 *Jagdgeschwader* involved was allocated one or more specific targets. JG 2's objective was St Trond, in Belgium, which had been a Luftwaffe nightfighter base for much of the war. Using aerial photographs and sand table models, Oberstleutnant Bühligen and his three *Gruppenkommandeure* briefed their pilots. Given the latter's almost complete inexperience, and the imposition of strict radio silence, the commanders' instructions amounted to little more than, 'Form up and follow me'.

For one young pilot of 11. *Staffel* even this proved too much. Only minutes after the 0800 hrs take-off from Altenstadt the Jumo engine of his 'long-nose' burst into flames and he crashed while still east of the Rhine – he was the first casualty of what was to be the *Jagdgeschwader 'Richthofen's'* blackest day.

Further losses followed soon after as the 90+ fighters of JG 2, joined by a gaggle of ground-attack Fw 190s flying down from Cologne, crossed the frontlines in the vicinity of Aachen. Over the next 37 miles (60 km) which separated them from their target, JG 2 lost more than a dozen fighters to Allied anti-aircraft fire. Among the machines hit was the Bf 109G-14 flown by the *Gruppenkommandeur* of II./JG 2. Hauptmann Georg Schröder parachuted into captivity near Verviers, in the Belgian Ardennes.

Worse was to come. Alerted by patrols already aloft, St Trond's defences were ready and waiting. As JG 2's fighters roared in low over the serried ranks of P-47s parked in rows about the field, they were met by a veritable hail of fire. Every weapon on the base seemed to be blazing away at them. Several of the attackers smashed into the ground immediately, while other pilots fought to gain height and were able to bail out.

With nearly a quarter of their number already lost, the *Geschwader* still had to get back to the dubious safety of their home bases. Allied defences, both on the ground and in the air, were by now fully aroused, and ensured that many didn't make it. The balance sheet would prove a sad epitaph for JG 2, as Operation *Bodenplatte* (Baseplate) – the 1945 New Year's Day attack on the Allied airfields – effectively sounded the death-knell of the *Jagdgeschwader 'Richthofen'* as a viable and cohesive fighting force:

Against the destruction of a handful of enemy fighters on the ground (St Trond's resident 48th and 404th FGs reported less than a dozen P-47s destroyed between them), JG 2 had lost no fewer than 33 pilots killed or missing (ten of whom were PoWs), plus another four wounded.

These casualties – totalling close on 40 per cent – would never be fully made good. It was a fortnight before JG 2 again participated in an operation of any size. In the interim a few replacement pilots had been drafted in, and the *Geschwader* (or what was left of it) had converted entirely on to Fw 190D-9s.

14 January 1945 witnessed the last major confrontation between the Luftwaffe and the Eighth Air Force over Germany. It finally broke the back of the *Jagdwaffe* in the west, the day costing the Luftwaffe's fighter units 139 casualties. Indicative of JG 2's depleted condition, out of this total, the unit's losses comprised just four 'long noses'.

Far removed from the grim realities of the fighting fronts, however, the Luftwaffe's organisational machinery continued to function smoothly.

The loss of Georg Schröder during *Bodenplatte* had promptly been made good by transferring Walter Matoni across from I. *Gruppe*. The new *Kommandeur* of II./JG 2 was awarded the Knight's Cross on 2 January.

I./JG 2 was placed in the hands of acting *Kommandeur* Hauptmann Fritz Karch, a long-serving member of the *Geschwader* who had joined 6. *Staffel* as a feldwebel in the autumn of 1942 (he had scored his first kills in Tunisia that November). But when Hauptmann Matoni was seriously injured in a crash-landing in February, Fritz Karch returned as *Kommandeur* to II./JG 2, which he would lead until the final surrender.

A newcomer was brought in to command I. *Gruppe* after Karch's temporary stewardship. Knight's Cross holder Hauptmann Franz Hrdlicka, ex-*Staffelkapitän* of 5./JG 77, had been wounded in a dogfight with Spitfires near Arnhem back in September. Now recovered, he arrived at Merzhausen with 44 victories to his credit. While *Kommandeur* of I./JG 2, Hrdlicka added at least one more kill to his score before receiving the Oak Leaves on 23 March. Forty-eight hours later he was shot down by US fighters north-east of Frankfurt.

By this time the *Geschwader* had flown its last few understrength missions as a bona fide 'multi-level' frontline unit. On 25 February two D-9s were lost to the fighter escort of a high-flying formation of Eighth Air Force B-24s east of Darmstadt, and five more Fw 190D-9 'long noses' fell to Ninth Air Force P-38s and P-47s escorting B-26 'mediums' near Mainz on 2 March.

Within the week the Focke-Wulfs were themselves employed in the bombing role, reportedly being sent in at low-level to attack the Ameri-

Possibly photographed at Ansbach, in Bavaria, in April 1945 (note the P-51D of the Ninth Air Force's 354th FG in the background), this burnt-out hulk of a Fw 190D-9 is reportedly the remains of a machine from JG 2

This 'long-nose' is also reputed to be a *'Richthofen'* aircraft. But are those aft fuselage bands, bisected by a III. *Gruppe* vertical bar, really yellow-white-yellow (they certainly appear much paler in other photographs of this same machine). Whatever its identity, let this solitary wreck – pictured in a forest 'somewhere in Germany' in the spring of 1945 – serve as a memorial to the 750+ pilots of the *Jagdgeschwader 'Richthofen'* reported killed or missing in action during World War 2

can-held bridge across the Rhine at Remagen with 250-kg (550-lb) bombs.

By early April JG 2 had been officially incorporated into *Luftflotte Reich*. Perhaps it was at this juncture that the *Geschwader's* Fw 190D-9s – all serviceable 16 of them – were given those controversial aft fuselage stripes.

Their tour of duty in defence of the rapidly shrinking perimeters of the Reich did not last long. JG 2's last move, in the closing weeks of the war, took them eastwards, via Bavaria, into the Protectorate of Bohemia, part of the one-time Czechoslovakia. It is ironic that arguably the most famous western front *Jagdgeschwader* of the entire Luftwaffe should end its operational career as it had begun it – in the east (the transfer to ex-Czech territory was the first time JG 2 had appeared on the 'eastern' front since 1. *Staffel's* abortive excursion into Polish airspace six years earlier).

It was at the time of the move into Bohemia that III. *Gruppe* disappeared from the scene. Some sources state that Hauptmann Siegfried Lemke led his surviving pilots up into the northern half of the now divided Germany (US and Soviet forces had met along the River Elbe on 25 April). But there is no record of III./JG 2 on any of the final orders of battle for May of those Luftwaffe *Divisionen* situated in the north.

Meanwhile, Oberstleutnant Bühligen and his remaining two *Gruppen* dutifully transferred eastwards. They now formed part of *Luftwaffenkommando 8*, and had been assigned to the rump of *IX. Fliegerkorps (J)*. This once-powerful all-jet command had by this late stage been reduced to just the *Geschwaderstab* and III. *Gruppe* of JG 7. It was to protect this handful of Me 262s, currently based at Prague-Ruzyn, that JG 2 was sent in to nearby airfields, Bühligen's *Stab* and Hauptmann Karch's II. *Gruppe* to Eger, and I./JG 2 (commanded since the loss of Hrdlicka by Oberleutnant Eickhoff) to Karlsbad.

This latest – and last – role for the *Geschwader* was even briefer than its previous weeks' 'Defence of the Reich'. The end of the war in Europe was only days away, and one of the final orders to emanate from *General der Flieger* Hans Seidemann, GOC *Lw.Kdo. 8* at Pardubitz, was for the disbandment of the *Geschwaderstab* and I. *Gruppe* of JG 2, and the transfer of II. *Gruppe* to Prague.

Instead, *Kommodore* Bühligen and Fritz Karch – the latter having been awarded JG 2's last Knight's Cross on, or about, 17 April – led the remains of the *Geschwader* back into Bavaria. It was here, as the armoured spearheads of General Patton's 3rd Army approached the small field outside Straubing, on the banks of the Danube, that JG 2's last dozen 'long-noses' were put to the torch.

The 11-year history of *Jagdgeschwader 2 'Richthofen'*, the Third Reich's premier fighter unit, showpiece of Göring's pre-war Luftwaffe, long-time masters of the French coast from the Seine to the Biscay and victors in some 2700 air combats, was at an end.

APPENDICES

APPENDIX 1

COMMANDING OFFICERS

Kommodores* of the *Jagdgeschwader 'Richthofen'

Raithel, *Maj* Johann	1/4/36	to	8/6/36
von Massow, *Oberst* Gerd	9/6/36	to	31/3/40
von Bülow-Bothkamp, *Oberst* Harry	1/4/40	to	2/9/40
Schellmann, *Maj* Wolfgang	3/9/40	to	19/10/40
Wick, *Maj* Helmut	20/10/40	to	28/11/40 (+)
Greisert, *Hptm* Karl-Heinz (acting)	29/11/40	to	15/2/41
Balthasar, *Hptm* Wilhelm	16/2/41	to	3/7/41 (+)
Oesau, *Obstlt* Walter	7/41	to	6/43
Mater, *Obstlt* Egon	1/7/43	to	2/3/44 (+)
Ubben, *Maj* Kurt	3/44	to	27/4/44 (+)
Bühligen, *Obstlt* Kurt	5/44	to	5/45

Gruppenkommandeure

I./JG 2 (and predecessors)

von Greim, *Maj* Robert Ritter	1/4/34	to	1/4/35
von Doering, *Maj* Kurt	1/4/35	to	1/4/36
Vieck, *Maj* Carl	1/4/36	to	17/10/39
Roth, *Hptm* Jürgen	17/10/39	to	22/6/40
Strümpell, *Hptm* Hennig	22/6/40	to	7/9/40
Wick, *Hptm* Helmut	7/9/40	to	20/10/40
Krahl, *Hptm* Karl-Heinz	20/10/40	to	20/11/41
Prestele, *Hptm* Ignaz	20/11/41	to	4/5/42
Leie, *Olt* Erich	4/5/42	to	1/43
Bolz, *Hptm* Helmut	1/43	to	5/43
Hohagen, *Maj* Erich	5/43	to	28/9/44
Matoni, *Hptm* Walter	9/44	to	12/44
Karch, *Hptm* Franz (acting)	12/44	to	2/45
Hrdlicka, *Hptm* Franz	2/45	to	25/3/45 (+)
Eickhoff, *Oblt*	26/3/45	to	5/45

(+) – Killed in action

II./JG 2 (and predecessors)

Raithel, *Maj* Johann	1/4/35	to	1/4/36
von Schoenebeck, *Maj* Karl-August	1/4/36	(into I./141)	
Schellmann, *Hptm* Wolfgang	11/39	to	2/9/40
Greisert, *Hptm* Karl-Heinz	2/9/40	to	1/5/42
Bolz, *Hptm* Helmut	1/5/42	to	12/42
Dickfeld, *Hptm* Adolf	12/42	to	1/43
Rudorffer, *Olt* Erich (Acting)	1/43	to	5/43
Rudorffer, *Hptm* Erich	5/43	to	8/43
Bühligen, *Hptm* Kurt	8/43	to	5/44
Schröder, *Hptm* Georg	5/44	to	1/1/45 (PoW)
Matoni, *Hptm* Walter	1/1/45	to	2/45
Karch, *Hptm* Franz	2/45	to	5/45

III./JG 2 (and predecessors)

Bormann, *Maj*	1/7/38	(into II./141)	
Mix, *Maj* Dr Erich	3/40	to	23/9/40
Bertram, *Olt* Otto	23/9/40	to	28/10/40
Hahn, *Maj* Hans	29/10/40	to	11/42
Mayer, *Hptm* Egon	11/42	to	30/6/43
Stolle, *Hptm* Bruno	1/7/43	to	3/44
Huppertz, *Hptm* Herbert	3/44	to	8/6/44 (+)
Wurmheller, *Hptm* Josef	8/6/44	to	22/6/44 (+)
Lemke, *Hptm* Siegfried	7/44	to	5/45

IV./JG 132

Osterkamp, *Maj* Theo	1/7/38	(into I./331)	

IV.(N)/JG 2

Blumensaat, *Hptm*	2/40	(into II./NJG 1)	

APPENDIX 2

AWARD WINNERS

All JG 2 winners of the Knight's Cross, and its higher grades, are presented here chronologically, with their scores at the time of the award(s) noted in brackets

	Knight's Cross		Oak Leaves		Swords	
von Bulow-Bothkamp, *Obstlt* Harry	22/8/40	(0)				
Wick, *Olt/Maj* Helmut	27/8/40	(20)	6/10/40	(42)		
Machold, *Ofw* Werner	5/9/40	(21)				
Schellmann, *Maj* Wolfgang	18/9/40	(10)				
Hahn, *Olt/Hptm* Hans	24/9/40	(20)	14/8/41	(42)		
Bertram, *Hptm* Otto	28/10/40	(13)				
Schnell, *Lt* Siegfried	9/11/40	(20)	9/7/41	(40)		
Krahl, *Hptm* Karl-Heinz	13/11/40	(15)				
Rudorffer, *Lt* Erich	1/5/41	(19)				
Balthasar, *Hptm* Wilhelm	2/7/41	(40)				
Mayer, *Lt/Hptm* Egon	1/8/41	(20)	16/4/43	(63)	2/3/44	(102)
Leie, *Olt* Erich	1/8/41	(21)				
Pflanz, *Olt* Rudolf	1/8/41	(20)				
Bühligen, *Ofw/Maj* Kurt	4/9/41	(21)	2/3/44	(96)	14/8/44	(104)
Wurmheller, *Ofw/Lt* Josef	4/9/41	(24)	13/11/42	(60)	24/10/44	(102)*
Liesendahl, *Hptm* Frank	4/9/42	(?)*				
Schröter, *Olt* Fritz	24/9/42	(7)				
Stolle, *Olt* Bruno	17/3/43	(29)				
Goltzsch, *Olt* Kurt	5/2/44	(43)*				
Lemke, *Lt* Siegfried	14/6/44	(47)				
Huppertz, *Hptm* Herbert	24/6/44	(68)*				
Hrdlicka, *Olt* Franz	9/8/44	(44)				
Matoni, *Hptm* Walter	2/1/45	(44?)				
Karch, *Hptm* Franz	17/4/45	(47?)				

* – Posthumous

APPENDIX 3

SERVING PILOTS OF JG 2 WITH 50+ WESTERN KILLS

	Kills In West	Four-Engined Bombers	Wartime Total (Inc East Front)
Bühligen, *Obstlt*, Kurt	112*	(24)	112
Mayer, *Obstlt*, Egon	102	(25)	102
Lemke, *Hptm*, Siegfried	95*	(21)	96
Wurmheller, *Hptm*, Josef	93**	(13+)	102
Schnell, *Hptm*, Siegfried	87**	(3)	93
Rudorffer, *Maj*, Erich	74*	(10)	222
Oesau, *Obstlt*, Walter	73**	(10)	115***
Hahn, *Maj*, Hans	68	(4)	108
Wick, *Maj*, Helmut	56		56
Pflanz, *Hptm*, Rudolf	52		52

* – including Mediterranean theatre ** – including some with other western *Jagdgeschwader* *** – plus 8 with *Legion Condor*

APPENDIX 4

REPRESENTATIVE ORDERS OF BATTLE

1/9/39

***Lfl.1/Luftgaukommando III* (Berlin)**			***Est/Serv***
Stab JG 2	Döberitz	Bf 109E	3 - 3
I./JG 2	Döberitz	Bf 109E	41 - 40
10.(N)/JG 2	Strausberg	Bf 109D	9 - 9
			Totals: 53 - 52

10/5/40

***Lfl.2/Jafü 'Deutsche Bucht'* (Jever)**			
IV.(N)/JG 2 (excluding 11.)	Hopsten	Bf 109D	19 - 18
		Ar 68	36 - 13
			Totals: 55 - 31
***Lfl.2/Fl.Fü.Drontheim* (Trondheim)**			
11.(N)/JG 2	Trondheim-Vaernes	Bf 109D	12 - 12
***Lfl.2/Jafü 2* (Dortmund)**			
II./JG 2	Münster	Bf 109E	47 - 35
***Lfl.3/Jafü 3* (Wiesbaden)**			
Stab JG 2	Wengerohr	Bf 109E	4 - 4
I./JG 2	Bassenheim	Bf 109E	45 - 33
III./JG 2	Freschweiler	Bf 109E	42 - 11
			Totals: 91 - 48

13/8/40

***Lfl.3/Jafü 3* (Deauville)**			
Stab JG 2	Beaumont-le-Roger	Bf 109E	3 - 3
I./JG 2	Beaumont-le-Roger	Bf 109E	34 - 32
II./JG 2	Beaumont-le-Roger	Bf 109E	36 - 28
III./JG 2	Le Havre/Octeville	Bf 109E	32 - 28
			Totals: 105 - 91

3/5/41

***Lfl.3/Jafü 3* (Deauville)**			
Stab JG 2	Beaumont-le-Roger	Bf 109F	6 - 5
I./JG 2	Cherbourg-Théville	Bf 109E/F	39 - 34
II./JG 2	Le Havre/Octeville	Bf 109E	30 - 28
III./JG 2	Le Havre/Octeville	Bf 109E/F	27 - 22
			Totals: 102 - 89

30/5/42

***Lfl/3/Jafü 3* (Deauville)**			
Stab JG 2	Beaumont-le-Roger	Bf 109G	4 - 2
Stabsschwarm JG 2	Ligescourt	Bf 109G	6 - 5
I./JG 2 (excluding 1. & 2.)	Triqueville	Bf 109G	12 - 6
1. & 2./JG 2	Ligescourt	Bf 109G	18 - 14
II./JG 2 (excluding 6.)	Beaumont-le-Roger	Fw 190A	34 - 27
6./JG 2	Triqueville	Fw 190A	12 - 11
III./JG 2 (excluding 7. & 8.)	Cherbourg-Théville	Fw 190A	13 - 12

			Est/Serv
7./JG 2	Morlaix	Fw 190A	10 - 8
8./JG 2	St Brieuc	Fw 190A	12 - 8
10.(*Jabo*)/JG 2	Caen-Carpiquet	Bf 109F	19 - 14
			Totals: 140 - 107
10/3/43			
***Lfl.3/Jafü 3* (Deauville)**			
Stab JG 2	Beaumont-le-Roger	Bf 109G	8 - 6
I./JG 2	Triqueville	Fw 190A	35 - 30
		Bf 109G	9 - 5
III./JG 2	Vannes	Fw 190A	63 - 39
10.(*Jabo*)/JG 2	St André-de-l'Eure	Fw 190A	- / -
12./JG 2	Bernay	Bf 109G	14 - 7
			Totals: 129 - 87
***Lfl.2/Fl.Fü. Afrika* (Tunis)**			
II./JG 2	Kairouan	Fw 190A	10 - 7
3/4/44			
***Lfl.3/Jafü 5* (Jouy-en-Josas)**			
Stab JG 2	Cormeilles	Fw 190A	6 - 1
II./JG 2	Creil	Bf 109G	43 - 16
III./JG 2	Cormeilles	Fw 190A	25 - 10
			Totals: 74 - 27
***Lfl.3/Jafü Südfrankreich* (Aix)**			
I./JG 2 (Part)	Aix	Fw 190/Bf 109	- / -
***Lfl.2/J.Abschn.Fü. Süd* (Torre Gaia)**			
I./JG 2 (Part)	Diabolo/Canino	Fw 109/Bf 109	- / -
26/7/44			
***Lfl. 3/5. Jagddivision* (Jouy-en-Josas)**			
Stab JG 2	Creil	Fw 190A	5 - 3
(I./JG 2	Husum	re-equipping)	
II./JG 2	Creil	Bf 109G	28 - 8
III./JG 2	Creil	Fw 190A	33 - 12
			Totals: 66 - 23
15/10/44			
***Lw.Kdo.West/5. Jagddivision* (Flammersfeld)**			
Stab JG 2	Nidda	Fw 190A	3 - 2
I./JG 2	Merzhausen	Fw 190A	36 - 21
II./JG 2	Nidda	Bf 109G	27 - 16
(III./JG 2	Königsberg in der Neumark	re-equipping)	
			Totals: 66 - 39
9/4/45			
***Lfl. Reich/15. Fliegerdivision* (?)**			
Stab JG 2	(Bavaria?)	Fw 190D	0 - 0
I./JG 2	(Bavaria?)	Fw 190D	5 - 3
II./JG 2	(Bavaria?)	Fw 190D	8 - 4
III./JG 2	(Bavaria?)	Fw 190D	12 - 9
			Totals: 25 - 16

COLOUR PLATES

1

Ar 65F 'D-IQIP' of *Fliegergruppe* Döberitz, Döberitz, April 1935

The Arado Ar 65E was first delivered to the *Reklamestaffel Mitteldeutschlands* towards the end of 1933. The improved F-model, which differed only in minor respects, was introduced the following year, and together with the E, formed the initial equipment of the *Fliegergruppe* Döberitz. The Luftwaffe's earliest markings, as shown here, comprised a civilian-style five-letter code. The 'D' ahead of the hyphen indicated Deutschland, the 'I' following it was the aircraft classification (single-engined, maximum weight 5000 kg) and the 'last three' (here 'QIP') denoted the machine's individual identity. Until September 1935 the starboard side of the vertical tail surfaces of all Luftwaffe aircraft carried red, white and black stripes – the colours of Imperial Germany. The white fuselage band applied to this machine is believed to signify a formation leader.

2

He 51A-1 '21+E13' of I./JG 132, Döberitz, July 1936

Fifteen months have passed, and the Döberitz *Gruppe's* title, equipment and markings have all undergone a change. This Heinkel He 51 bears the alpha-numeric code system introduced on 1 June 1936. The '21' to the left of the fuselage cross identifies JG 132, the aircraft's individual identity is now provided by the letter ('E') immediately to the right of the cross, and the last two numbers are those of the *Gruppe* (I) and *Staffel* (3.), respectively. The swastika now adorns both sides of the tailfin and rudder, and the nose sports JG 132's new red trim.

3

He 51B-1 'White 12' of II./JG 132, Jüterbog-Damm, October 1936

The alpha-numeric code system shown above proved totally unsuitable for rapid air-to-air identification. On 1 September 1936 a completely new style of high-visibility markings was introduced on Luftwaffe fighters. Using white geometric symbols (chevrons, bars etc.) allied to large individual aircraft numerals, this system formed the basis for all future Luftwaffe fighter markings right up until the end of the war. Here, the horizontal bar behind the '12' indicates II. *Gruppe* and the circles denote that this aircraft belongs to the *Gruppe's* third *Staffel* (i.e. 6./JG 132). Note how the red trim has been extended along the spine, and also forms an aft fuselage band to make the rear circle more easily visible.

4

Bf 109B-2 'Red 3' of II./JG 132, Jüterbog-Damm, August 1937

When II. *Gruppe* took delivery of their first Bf 109s, the new monoplane's drab camouflage heralded further changes in markings. The individual aircraft numeral and II. *Gruppe* horizontal bar were now positioned immediately in front of, and behind, the fuselage cross respectively. *Staffel* symbols were dispensed with, being replaced by colour-coding (each *Gruppe's* first, second and third *Staffeln* initially being identified by white, red and yellow). Finally, with the colourful trims of the biplane era fast disappearing, the only clue to a parent *Geschwader's* identity was provided by the emerging crop of new badges and emblems – as seen here with JG 132's red script 'R', for 'Richthofen', on a silver shield.

5

Ar 68E 'Black Chevron' of *Stab* III./JG 132, Fürstenwalde, September 1938

Although formed from three hitherto semi-autonomous Ar 68 *Staffeln* in the weeks leading up to the Sudeten crisis, III./JG 132 nevertheless found the time to apply a textbook set of markings to each of its Arado biplanes. This particular machine displays not only a standard III. *Gruppe* 'wavy' bar, but also the single chevron of an adjutant. Believed to be the mount of Leutnant Riegel (who later flew with I./ZG 76), the pilot's position as No 2 to the *Gruppenkommandeur* is further confirmed by the numeral between the chevron and bar, this and the spinner tip being applied in the official *Stab* colour of green.

6

He 112B-0 'Yellow 5' of IV./JG 132, Leipzig, September 1938

One of several areas of doubt in the *Geschwader's* history that is still to be clarified is IV./JG 132's use of a *Staffel* of 'impressed' Heinkel He 112 fighters (being readied for export to Japan) at the time of the Sudeten crisis. Photographs of such machines in standard Luftwaffe finish and markings of the period (albeit minus the IV. *Gruppe* disc one would expect to see aft of the fuselage cross) were certainly taken – and published – but were they actually being operated by the Luftwaffe, or simply being used as a propaganda ploy to confound the Allies?

7

Bf 109D 'White 11' of 10.(N)/JG 2, Strausberg, September 1939

On the outbreak of war the Bf 109Ds of Oberleutnant Blumensaat's nightfighting 10. *Staffel* wore the standard two-tone green finish of the period – only the large 'N' (for *Nacht*) behind the fuselage cross indicated their actual role. Many of these machines were photographed minus their cockpit canopies (as here), and a number of sources state that they were flown in this fashion – or just with the roof glazing removed – to reduce reflected searchlight glare. Note, too, the amended tail markings, now consisting simply of a swastika centred on the rudder hinge line.

8

Bf 109E-1 'White 5' of Leutnant Paul Temme, 1./JG 2, Döberitz, September 1939

Wearing almost identical finish and markings to the machine featured in the previous profile (but without the 'N', of course), this early *Emil* belongs to 1./JG 2, which was the only *Staffel* to see brief action during the Polish campaign. Pilot Paul Temme later became Adjutant of I. *Gruppe*, only to be shot down over West Sussex early on the morning of *'Adlertag'*, 13 August 1940.

9

Bf 109E-3 'Chevron-Triangle' of Major Dr Erich Mix, *Gruppenkommandeur* III./JG 2, France, May 1940

This machine offers an example not only of the predominantly *hellblau* (light blue-grey) finish first introduced during the winter of 1939-40, but also of the less common 'outline only' style of rank and *Gruppe* markings. Dr Mix, who had achieved three victories in World War 1, opened his score in the second conflict by claiming a pair of French Morane fighters during the 'Phoney War' (while serving with I./JG 53). These are duly marked on the rudder of this aircraft, which he forced-landed near Roye on 21 May. Although Dr Mix subsequently became *Kommodore* of JG 1 (1942-43), before being elevated to *Jafü Bretagne* in December 1943, previous reports that he gained a total of 13 World War 2 victories now appear doubtful.

10

Bf 109E-3 'Yellow 8' of Leutnant Rudolf Rothenfelder, 9./JG 2, Le Havre/Octeville, August 1940

The Battle of Britain was not many weeks old before the previously pristine *hellblau* flanks of the *Geschwader's Emils* began to be toned-down by a variety of hand-applied dapple camouflage finishes. 'Yellow 8' also sports 9. *Staffel's* newly-introduced *Stechmücke* (Gnat) badge. This was designed by 'Rudi' Rothenfelder, who had previously served with I./JG 20 in Poland. One of the unsung 'rank-and-filers' who constituted the backbone of every fighter unit, Rothenfelder survived the war, most of it having been spent with JG 2.

11

Bf 109E-3 'White 8' of Oberfeldwebel Kurt Goltzsch, 7./JG 2, Cherbourg-Théville, September 1940

Another III. *Gruppe* machine, this one bearing the white markings of 7. *Staffel* (including the spinner tip) and the unit's quasi-political 'Thumb pressing down Chamberlain's hat' badge. The latter was co-designed by Leutnant Schmidt and Oberfeldwebel Hans Klee. The most obvious difference between this *Emil* and the one above is the yellow nose and rudder, introduced at the end of August to improve air-to-air recognition. Kurt Goltzsch was another long-serving member of the *Geschwader*, rising to command 5. *Staffel*, and with 43 victories to his credit, before being severely wounded in September 1943. As a result of further injuries sustained in the ensuing forced-landing, Goltzsch died on 26 September 1944.

12

Bf 109E-4 'Red 1' of 8./JG 2, Oye-Plage, September 1940

The badge of III. *Gruppe's* remaining *Staffel* could claim a more heraldic provenance, being based on the family coat of arms of 8./JG 2's first *Staffelkapitän*, Hauptmann Alexander von Winterfeldt. It is seen here in its elaborate early form, complete with background shield, as carried at the time of the unit's brief deployment to the Pas de Calais at the beginning of September. 'Red 1' is almost certainly the mount of the then *Staffelkapitän*, Oberleutnant Bruno Stolle, who would assume command of III. *Gruppe* in July 1943.

13

Bf 109E-4 'Black Double Chevron' of Hauptmann Helmut Wick, *Gruppenkommandeur* of I./JG 2, Beaumont-le-Roger, October 1940

Pictured midway through its evolution from 'Yellow 2' to full *Kommodore's* markings, Wick's *Emil* wears a very dense (sponge-applied?) dapple finish and the toned-down form of fuselage cross much favoured by I. *Gruppe*. The emblem on the rather pale yellow cowling – long thought to be Wick's personal marking – is, in fact, the badge of 3./JG 2. Based on the pennant of a Pommeranian hunting club, and incorporating the huntsman's/fighter pilot's traditional *'Horrido'* victory cry, it was applied in blue and yellow in honour of the then *Kapitän* Hennig Strümpell's Swedish ancestry. Note that Wick's personal *'Vöglein'* (Little bird) emblem is, in fact, missing at this stage, possibly covered up by fresh dappling – it would later be obliterated entirely by the *Kommodore's* forward chevron.

14

Bf 109E-7 'White 15' of Oberleutnant Werner Machold, *Staffelkapitän* 7./JG 2, Caen-Rocquancourt, May 1941

Believed to be the machine in which Werner Machold forced-landed with a dead engine at Worth Matravers, west of Swanage, on 9 June 1941, this *Emil* has the distinctive pointed spinner cap of the E-7 variant and carries a 250-kg (550-lb) bomb on its ventral rack. As well as the *Staffel* badge on the cowling, it also features a precise record of Machold's 32 kills on the rudder. The first six of his victories were French, the remainder British – the last two were a pair of Spitfires (almost certainly from No 234 Sqn, which in actuality lost a single aircraft on this day) claimed north of Weymouth on 19 May.

15

Bf 109F-2 'White Double Chevron' of Hauptmann Hans Hahn, *Gruppenkommandeur* III./JG 2, St Pol, Summer 1941

Machold's E-7 was the last *Emil* lost by III./JG 2, for the *Geschwader* had, by this time, been almost completely re-equipped with the new and improved Bf 109F, or *Friedrich*. 'Assi' Hahn's F-2 wears standard finish and markings of the period, plus the new 'Rooster's head' *Gruppe* badge. This latter was a play on the *Kommandeur's* name, for Hahn meaning 'cockerel' in German. Another innovation from this period was the replacement of III. *Gruppe's* 'wavy bar' with a plain vertical bar, although in the case of the *Stab's* aircraft this was extended to form a narrow band completely encircling the rear fuselage.

16

Bf 109F-2 'White 1' of Oberleutnant Egon Mayer, *Staffelkapitän* 7./JG 2, St Pol, Summer 1941

The *Friedrich* of one of 'Assi' Hahn's *Staffelkapitäne* exhibits the standard style of III. *Gruppe* vertical bar. Wearing a distinctly darker dapple than the pevious machine, 'White 1' displays three other differences – the absence of the famous 'Red R' *Geschwader* badge (which was now to be removed from all operational aircraft by official edict), the restriction of the Channel Front yellow nose markings to just the lower nacelle panels and the attachment of a *Staffelkapitän's* metal pennant (bearing 7./JG 2's badge in miniature) to the aerial mast.

17

Bf 109F-4 'Black Chevron and Bars' of Major Walter Oesau, *Geschwaderkommodore* JG 2, St.Pol, Autumn 1941

There would be little to indicate that this otherwise

anonymous and rather nondescript *Friedrich* belongs to one of the *Jagdwaffe's* true 'greats', were it not for the *Kommodore's* markings. These are based on the original 1936 pattern of a forward chevron, combined with a horizontal bar on either side of the fuselage cross. In fact, as one of a *Kommodore's* little perks, 'Gulle' Oesau had two almost identical F-4s kept at his disposal. And although by the end of September 1941 he was just two short of his century, there were no victory marks of any kind to be seen on either machines' rudder.

18

Bf 109F-4 'Black Chevron and Crossed Bar(s)' of Oberleutnant Erich Leie, *Geschwader-Adjutant* JG 2, St Pol, Autumn 1941

Erich Leie served as Oesau's No 2, and as such his *Friedrich* was almost a carbon-copy of his *Geschwaderkommodore's* fighter(s). He, too, has eschewed any form of victory markings (by this time his score was rapidly approaching the 30 mark). Leie has, however, allowed himself one touch of individuality – he has chosen to combine the markings of a pre-war *Stabskette* No 2 (a horizontal bar each side of the fuselage cross) with the chevron and vertical bar of a wartime *Geschwader-Adjutant*, to produce this unusual, and possibly unique, set of insignia.

19

Bf 109F-4 'Black Bars and Dot' of Oberleutnant Rudolf Pflanz, *Geschwader-TO* JG 2, St Pol, Autumn 1941

The third member of a pre-war biplane *Stabskette* also displayed a horizontal bar each side of the fuselage cross, but with a small rectangular dot placed just above the leading bar. As the third man in Oesau's *Stabsschwarm*, Pflanz has opted for the same. Some sources maintain, however, that this was not Pflanz's regular aircraft (despite the impressive rudder tally), and that his machine carried wartime TO insignia of chevron, vertical bar and circle. Anything is possible, for as far as markings were concerned, JG 2's *Stabsschwarm* – which was later increased to six machines – appear to have been a law unto themselves.

20

Bf 109F-4 'Yellow 9' of Oberleutnant Erich Rudorffer, *Staffelkapitän* 6./JG 2, Abbeville-Drucat, Autumn 1941

Rudorffer's *Friedrich* provides an example of the less common combination of 71/02 upper surface camouflage colours. But note the striking discrepancy between the engine cowling and the rest of the aircraft, the former presumably being a replacement part (or perhaps the result of heavy-handed overspraying of a previously all-yellow cowling). The rudder carefully chronicles Rudorffer's victories to date – the first nine French and the following 30 all British (the last of which were a trio of Spitfires claimed on 21 September). By war's end Rudorffer's kills would total a staggering 222, making him the seventh-highest scoring ace of the entire *Jagdwaffe*!

21

Bf 109F-4/B 'Blue 1 Chevron and Bar' of Oberleutnant Frank Liesendahl, *Staffelkapitän* 10. (*Jabo*)/ JG 2, Beaumont-le-Roger, April 1942

An *Experte* of a different kind, who kept an equally meticulous record of his achievements, was Frank Liesendahl, *Kapitän* of the highly successful fighter-bomber *Staffel*. In fact this rudder – bearing the silhouettes of six freighters, totalling 27,500 BRT, sunk or damaged in the English Channel between May 1941 and March 1942 – had been transferred from an earlier 'Blue 1' at the time of the *Jabostaffel's* re-equipment from F-2s to F-4s. Liesendahl was killed attacking yet another merchantman off the Devon coast in July 1942.

22

Bf 109G-1 'White 11' of Oberleutnant Julius Meimberg, *Staffelkapitän* 11./JG 2, Poix, Summer 1942

In mid-May 1942 1. *Staffel* was sub-divided to form a new, specialised high-altitude *Staffel*, 11./JG 2, which was equipped with the first examples of Messerschmitt's new *Gustav*, the pressurised Bf 109G-1. The visible distinguishing features of this variant can just be made out on Meimberg's 'White 11' – the small inlet scoop for the air compressor above the supercharger intake, and the anti-condensation silica gel pellets inserted between the double-glazed cockpit panels. This 11. *Staffel* did not remain with the *Geschwader* for long, being incorporated into JG 53 after transferring to North Africa at the end of 1942.

23

Fw 190A-2 'Yellow 13' of Oberfeldwebel Josef Heinzeller, 3./JG 2, Triqueville, June 1942

It was not common for the *Geschwader's* aircraft to carry personal markings (Wick's 'little bird' being one obvious exception), but the emblem and name adorning the cowling of one of I./JG 2's earliest Focke-Wulfs go back a long way. They first appeared on Heinzeller's Bf 109E, of I.(J)/LG 2, during the Polish campaign, and were reportedly applied in honour both of his pet scottie and his wife (although the addition of the name *Old Shap* beneath the cockpit of the present machine would seem to suggest that he had since transferred his affections from at least one or the other of the above!). Unlike its pilot, who survived the war, Wk-Nr 325 was later written-off in a crash-landing after being relegated to a training unit.

24

Fw 190A-3 'Black Bars and Crossbar' of Leutnant Hubert von Greim, *Stab* JG 2, Triqueville, Summer 1942

The *Geschwaderstab's* addiction to idiosyncratic insignia survived reactivation and the conversion to Fw 190s, for the unusual markings depicted here had been sported by a *Friedrich* based at St Pol and Beaumont during the preceding year. Von Greim, who was the son of *Fliegergruppe* Döberitz's first *Kommandeur* back in 1934 (and, 11 years later, the second and last C-in-C of the Luftwaffe after the dismissal of the disgraced Göring in the closing days of the war) was not the only bearer of a famous family name to appear on JG 2's pilot roster – Oberleutnant Wolf von Bülow, Leutnant Walter Göring and Oberfähnrich Ruthart von Richthofen were all killed while serving with the *Geschwader*.

25

Fw 190A-3 'Yellow 1' of Oberleutnant Erich Rudorffer, *Staffelkapitän* 6./JG 2, Beaumont-le-Roger, August 1942

Almost a year has passed since the time of Erich Rudorffer's *Friedrich*, 'Yellow 9', featured as profile 20.

During that period he has acquired a new aircraft and six more victories to add to his rudder scoreboard. Strangely, the top row of individual – French? – kills now seems to have grown to ten. Shortly after this Rudorffer was severely wounded. His subsequent hospitalisation delayed his departure for Tunisia, where his rise to fame would really begin to accelerate.

26

Fw 190A-3 'White Double Chevron' of Hauptmann Hans Hahn, *Gruppenkommandeur* III./JG 2, Poix, September 1942

Offering the opportunity to compare another well-known pilot's transition from *Friedrich* to Focke-Wulf, 'Assi' Hahn's new mount bears very similar markings to those depicted earlier (in profile 15), although the angle of the white *Kommandeur's* chevrons is now decidedly shallower. And while the *Geschwader* badge may have disappeared from beneath the cockpit – and the personal scoreboard from the rudder – the 'cockerel's head' soldiers on.

27

Fw 190A-4 'White 1' of Oberleutnant Kurt Bühligen, *Staffelkapitän* 4./JG 2, Kairouan/Tunisia, December 1942

This machine provides a good example of the finish and markings of II./JG 2's Focke-Wulfs upon their transfer to North Africa. Although still in standard northern European camouflage, and wearing the Channel front's yellow undercowling and rudder, bands of Mediterranean theatre white have already been applied around the aft fuselage and under the wings immediately outboard of the cross (perhaps to aid recognition during their transfer flight south through Italy). This aircraft was being piloted by 4. *Staffel's* Unteroffizier Erich Engelbrecht when it was shot down in combat with six USAAF Spitfires west of Kairouan on 8 March 1943.

28

Fw 190A-4 'Black Double Chevron' of Oberleutnant Adolf Dickfeld, *Gruppenkommandeur* II./JG 2, Kairouan/Tunisia, January 1943

In contrast to the previous Fw 190, the *Kommandeur's* machine is representative of the freshly-painted, unfaded desert tan finish being worn by many of the *Gruppe's* Focke-Wulfs within weeks of their arrival in Tunisia (although whether such aircraft were newly delivered in this scheme, or were in-theatre resprays is not clear). Note that whereas the aft fuselage band and white spinner tip have been retained, there are no white markings underwing. The overall dark appearance of these machines quickly faded under the hot North African sun.

29

Fw 190A-4 'Yellow 4' of Hauptmann Siegfried Schnell, *Staffelkapitän* of 9./JG 2, Vannes, February 1943

Far removed from the rigours of Tunisia, 'Wumm' Schnell's pristine A-4 displays a textbook set of Channel front markings (even if, at this particular juncture, 9. *Staffel* was on one of its frequent deployments to the Biscay coast). Schnell was another who kept careful record of his successes. Below the figure 40 and Knight's Cross depicted at the top of the rudder, there are a further 35 individual kill bars, the last four of which bear American stars to mark his first victories against the USAAF.

30

Fw 190A-4 'Black Rectangle and Bars' of Oberstleutnant Walter Oesau, *Geschwaderkommodore* JG 2, Beaumont-le-Roger, February 1943

In contrast to Schnell's colourful 'Anton-4', some 200 miles (320 km) to the east Walter Oesau was flying a machine which was plain to the point of anonymity – even the *Kommodore* markings of his earlier *Friedrichs*, not exactly flamboyant to begin with, had been pared down still further. The one splash of colour was the yellow undercowling, the only other feature being the black area aft of the nacelle – a decoration frequently employed by JG 2 to hide those 'unsightly exhaust stains' – and even this was of the simplest shape possible.

31

Fw 190A-4 'Black 1' of Oberleutnant Horst Hannig, *Staffelkapitän* 2./JG 2, Triqueville, Spring 1943

Going to the other extreme, Horst Hannig's 'Black 1' is adorned with one of the more elaborate motifs applied to disguise the soot deposits which quickly collected behind the Focke-Wulf's exhaust louvres. This striking 'Eagle's head' design was more commonly associated with III. *Gruppe* machines, although many of the latter (including Schnell's 'Yellow 4' above) later repainted their engine cowlings, removing the eagle's head to make way for 'Assi' Hahn's far less intimidating cockerel.

32

Fw 190A-5 'White Double Chevron' of Hauptmann Egon Mayer, *Gruppenkommandeur* III./JG 2, Cherbourg-Théville, Spring 1943

Egon Mayer flew at least two identically-marked Focke-Wulfs while leading III. *Gruppe*, the A-4 of late 1942 (see cover painting) giving way to this A-5 in the early spring of 1943. Bearing more than a passing resemblance to Hahn's even earlier A-3 (see profile 26), both of Mayer's machines did, however, carry detailed rudder scoreboards. Here, the total is 62, including six US 'heavies' – just one more would earn Mayer the Oak Leaves to his Knight's Cross.

33

Fw 190A-4 'Green 13' of Oberstleutnant Walter Oesau, *Geschwaderkommodore* JG 2, Beaumont-le-Roger, June 1943

For a time during the mid-war years a number of *Jagdgeschwader* – JG 2 included – decided to dispense with *Stab* symbols (presumably the distinctive chevrons and bars were making the formation leaders too easily identifiable to canny Allied fighter pilots). In their place, *Stab* machines were given numerals – usually in the twenties (regular *Staffel* machines were rarely numbered above the mid-teens at this period). But Oesau, ever the individualist, has opted for '13', and reportedly in green (thinly outlined in yellow), despite the official *Geschwaderstab* colours being blue. He has, however, conformed to regulations with a yellow rudder, which remains steadfastly bare of any sign of his 100+ victories.

34

Fw 190A-6 'Yellow 2' of Oberleutnant Josef Wurmheller, *Staffelkapitän* 9./JG 2, Vannes, September 1943

'Sepp' Wurmheller was Siegfried Schnell's immediate

successor as *Staffelkapitän* of the Vannes-based 9./JG 2. It is hardly surprising, therefore, that their two aircraft (see profile 29) bear very similar markings. Apart from the individual aircraft letter, the main difference is in the absence of the long-serving 'cockerel's head' *Gruppe* badge (III./JG 2 was now in the capable hands of Bruno Stolle). Less immediately obvious are the differing rudder scoreboard details, Wurmheller's displaying the '60', which won him the Oak Leaves, plus a further 21 individual victory bars.

35

Bf 109G-6 'White 2' of 4./JG 2, Evreux, Autumn 1943

Following its return from Tunisia in the spring of 1943 II. *Gruppe* converted back on to the Bf 109. This heavily-dappled *Gustav*, armed with underwing cannon gondolas (such aircraft being colloquially known as *'Kanonenboote'*, or 'gunboats'), was typical of the finish and markings of this period. As far as is known, II./JG 2 never carried any identifying *Gruppe* or *Staffel* badges. The earlier decree banning the use of the *Geschwader* emblem had thus rendered them virtually anonymous for a good two-thirds of the war.

36

Bf 109G-6 'Blue 6' of 8./JG 2, Creil, April 1944

Another of II./JG 2's incognito *Gustav* 'gunboats' depicted in the weeks leading up to the invasion of Normandy. By this time the *Gruppe* had been expanded to four *Staffeln*. As the new addition, 8./JG 2 (the ex-12. *Staffel*) carried blue individual aircraft numbers and *Gruppe* bar.

37

Fw 190A-8 'Black Double Chevron and Bars' of Major Bühligen, *Geschwaderkommodore* JG 2, Creil June 1944

In keeping with the *Geschwaderstab's* long-standing tradition of individualism and non-conformity, Major Bühligen's A-8 wears a most unusual finish and set of markings (the latter reportedly introduced by Kurt Ubben in the spring of 1944). In addition to the splinter camouflage and unique double chevron, note the spiral spinner and the bizarre presentation of the tailfin swastika.

38

Bf 109G-14 'Black 8' of 5./JG 2, Ettingshausen, December 1944

Back to the anonymity of II. *Gruppe* with this Erla-canopied, tall-tail Bf 109G-14 of late 1944. This profile, reconstructed from photographs of a damaged *Gustav* found abandoned at Ettingshausen (one of II./JG 2's two main bases in the winter of 1944-45), almost certainly features a 'Richthofen' machine – an assumption borne out by the plain horizontal bar aft of the fuselage cross (all three other Bf 109G-equipped II. *Gruppen* in the west at this time are known to have worn Defence of the Reich bands).

39

Fw 190D-9 'Yellow 11' of II./JG 2, Stockheim, March 1945

By the early weeks of 1945 II./JG 2 had once again reverted to the Fw 190 (this time of the 'long-nose' variety), thus bringing them into line with the rest of the *Geschwader*. Again based on photographs of a wrecked machine (found on a small airstrip some six miles due south of Nidda), the aircraft depicted in this profile undoubtedly wore Defence of Reich bands – and they were reportedly yellow-white-yellow (note how the break in the white band has been used to create a II. *Gruppe* horizontal bar). This is the only kind of evidence to date to suggest – contrary to some other sources – that the RV bands assigned to JG 2 were, in fact, actually applied to their Focke-Wulfs.

40

Fw 190D-9 'White 4' of JG 2, Straubing, May 1945

It would be naive to suggest that JG 2 spent the last few chaotic days of their existence – as the Third Reich collapsed about them – applying and removing fuselage stripes according to the dictates of which particular command they happened to be serving under: *Luftflotte Reich* or Lw.Kdo. 8. This third and final profile, based upon wreckage discovered and photographed by members of General Patton's 3rd Army, is perforce more representational than profiles 38 and 39. What can be stated with certainty is that the said wreckage was found at Straubing, JG 2's last known resting place, and that the *Geschwader's* final dozen D-9s would have looked very similar to the aircraft depicted here.

BIBLIOGRAPHY

BINGHAM, VICTOR, *Blitzed! The Battle of France May - June 1940.* Air Research Publications, New Malden, 1990

CONSTABLE, TREVOR J and TOLIVER, COL RAYMOND F, *Horrido! Fighter Aces of the Luftwaffe.* Macmillan, New York, 1968

CULL, BRIAN et al, *Twelve Days in May: The Air Battle for Northern France and the Low Countries 10-21 May 1940.* Grub Street, London, 1995

DIERICH, WOLFGANG, *Die Verbände der Luftwaffe 1935-1945.* Motorbuch Verlag, Stuttgart, 1976

FRAPPE, JEAN-BERNARD, *La Luftwaffe face au débarquement allié.* Editions Heimdal, Bayeux, 1999

FREEMAN, ROGER A, *Mighty Eighth War Diary.* Jane's, London 1981

GAUL, W, *Die Deutsche Luftwaffe während der invasion 1944.* Arbeitskreis für Wehrforschung, 1953

GIRBIG, WERNER, *Start im Morgengrauen.* Motorbuch Verlag, Stuttgart, 1973

GREEN, WILLIAM, *Augsburg Eagle: The Story of the Messerschmitt 109.* Macdonald, London, 1971

GUNDELACH, KARL, *Drohende Gefahr West: Die deutsche Luftwaffe vor und während der Invasion 1944.* Arbeitskreis für Wehrforschung, 1959

HELD, WERNER, *Die deutsche Tagjagd.* Motorbuch Verlag, Stuttgart, 1977

MASON, FRANCIS K, *Battle over Britain.* McWhirter Twins, London, 1969

MEHNERT, KURT and TEUBER, REINHARD, *Die deutsche Luftwaffe 1939-1945.* Militär-Verlag Patzwall, Norderstedt, 1996

MIDDLEBROOK, MARTIN and EVERITT, CHRIS, *The Bomber Command War Diaries 1939-1945.* Penguin, London, 1990

MÖLLER-WITTEN, HANNS, *Mit dem Eichenlaub zum Ritterkreuz.* Erich Pabel Verlag, Rastatt, 1962

NAUROTH, HOLGER, *Jagdgeschwader 2 'Richthofen': Eine Bildchronik.* Motorbuch Verlag, Stuttgart, 1999

OBERMAIER, ERNST, *Die Ritterkreuzträger der Luftwaffe 1939-1945: Band I, Jagdflieger.* Verlag Dieter Hoffmann, Mainz, 1966

PARKER, DANNY S, *To Win the Winter Sky; Air War over the Ardennes 1944-1945.* Greenhill Books, London, 1994

PAYNE, MICHAEL, *Messerschmitt Bf 109 into the Battle.* Air Research Publications, Surbiton, 1987

PRIEN, JOCHEN/RODEIKE, PETER, *Messerschmitt Bf 109F, G and K Series.* Schiffer, Atglen 1993

PRICE, DR ALFRED, *The Luftwaffe Data Book.* Greenhill Books, London, 1997

RAMSEY, WINSTON G (ed), *The Battle of Britain Then and Now.* After the Battle, London, 1985

RAMSEY, WINSTON G (ed), *The Blitz Then and Now (3 Vols).* After the Battle, London, 1987-90

RODEIKE, PETER, *Focke-Wulf Jagdflugzeug: Fw 190A, Fw 190 'Dora', Ta 152H.* Rodeike, Eutin, 1999

SCHRAMM, PERCY ERNST (ed), *Die Niederlage 1945.* DTV, Munich, 1962

SCHRAMM, PERCY ERNST (ed), *Kriegstagebuch des OKW (8 Vols).* Manfred Pawlak, Herrsching, 1982

SHORES, CHRISTOPHER, et al, *Fighters over Tunisia.* Neville Spearman, London, 1975

SHORES, CHRISTOPHER, et al, *Fledgling Eagles.* Grub Street, London, 1991

SPAETHE, KARL-HEINZ, Der Rote Baron und seine tollkühnen Manner, blick + bild Verlag, Velbert, 1972

VÖLKER, KARL-HEINZ, *Die deutsche Luftwaffe 1933-1939.* Deutsche Verlags-Anstalt, Stuttgart, 1967

MAGAZINES, PERIODICALS AND ANNUALS
(VARIOUS ISSUES)

Adler, Der

Berliner Illustrierte Zeitung

Flugzeug

Jägerblatt

Jahrbuch der deutschen Luftwaffe

Jet & Prop

Militärhistorische Schriftenreihe

Signal

Wehrmacht, Die

Wehrwissenschaftliche Rundschau

INDEX

Figures in **bold** refer to illustrations